# The Plugged-In Parent

# The
# *Plugged-In*
# Parent

## What You Should Know About
## Kids and Computers

## *Steve Bennett*

TIMES BOOKS

RANDOM HOUSE

Library of Congress Cataloging-in-Publication Data

Bennett, Steven J., 1951–
The plugged-in parent / Steve Bennett. — 1st ed.
p.    cm.
ISBN 0-8129-6378-4
1. Internet (Computer network) and children.   2. Parenting.
3. Computers and family.   4. Family—Computer network
resources.   I. Title.
HQ784.I58B46      1998
649′.1—dc21                                              98-9514

Manufactured in the United States of America on acid-free paper
9  8  7  6  5  4  3  2
First Edition
Book design by Susan Hood

# Contents

# Contents

# Introduction:
# Of Dream Machines and
# Digital Demons

"My daddy owns a toy store on the computer." So reads the cover page of a "brochure" that my seven-year-old daughter, Audrey, made to cheer me up in the midst of a work crunch. I chuckled at the endearing copy that followed, touting the virtues of the online enterprise that my wife and I launched in early 1996. Then it struck me—for this child of the nineties, virtual stores were just another way to buy things and another way for dads to make a living. No big deal.

"Egads, doesn't she know this is incredible?" I think to myself. "Doesn't she realize that she's witnessing the greatest transformation of commerce since the industrial revolution? Doesn't she know that we're surfing on the cutting edge of technology, right here in our house?"

Of course not. Aside from the fact that she's just seven, technology has always been a part of her young life. She's a member, like her ten-year-old brother, Noah, of a digital generation that began banging on keyboards as toddlers and now can do things with PCs that would leave many adults scratching their heads.

But for all their technological prowess, will kids of the digital era fare better than their predecessors? Will computers and related technologies become dream machines that enhance kids' lives? Or will computers turn out to be digital demons that hasten the already-shrinking period of life known as childhood? The former, of course, would realize our best hopes as parents and educators for technology. The latter would indeed be sad, for without childhood, the wonder years simply become a hollow segue to adulthood.

At first blush, this might sound like a bit of nostalgia for the good old days when kids were just kids. It's not. This generation is growing up at an incredibly fast pace, with many youngsters sophisticated way beyond their years. The pressure is on for kids to think and act like adults at earlier and earlier ages. It seems that it's only when young peoples' behavior involves crime, substance abuse, or the consequences of sexual activity that we shake our heads in wonderment and reflect on how different things were when *we* were growing up. Only then do we realize that something seems to be missing, and that that something is childhood.

Ironically, as we become more technologically sophisticated, in some ways we're regressing in the way that we think of childhood. Prior to the mid-twentieth century, most people thought of children as miniature adults. Children were depicted that way in paintings and treated that way in terms of work. Our conception didn't really begin to change until psychologists like Jean Piaget pointed out that children aren't just little people who don't know as much as big people; their thought processes are qualitatively different as well. Now, as we head toward the new millennium, our pre-occupation with technology can push childhood further into the background. I believe that, when used properly, technology can empower children in many ways and give them a voice. But when kids suddenly abandon their long-term interests in music, sports, and various hobbies in favor of the machine, as many do, it's time for parents to take action and introduce balance into their kids' lives.

The burden falls on parents to ensure that technology enriches their children's lives, rather than displaces traditional low-tech/no-tech pursuits. As if parenting weren't difficult enough already! What with all the conventional hurdles we have to overcome, now we have to think about how technology affects our kids. This is complicated by the fact that we don't have any models to follow; there really aren't any precedents for the introduction of highly seductive and rapidly changing technology into our children's lives. Back in the fifties, when I was growing up, technology wasn't even on the parenting radar screen. Oh, I was told not to set up my electric train near the wash basins in the basement, not to sit too close to the TV (bad for the eyes), and *never* to stick a knife in the toaster. That was pretty much it for technology; once you learned the rules, the rules didn't change.

Today's computer technology, in contrast, is rapidly evolving, and the rules transform so fast we can't keep up with them. Look back to the start of the microcomputing revolution, and compare what you could do then and now. In the early eighties, computing essentially meant word processing, creating spreadsheets, generating simple charts and graphs, building databases, and performing (very slow) transfers of data. The games available in the early days were rudimentary at best and hardly of concern to parents.

Only the most farsighted visionaries back then could have dreamed of what technology users can do today, such as tuning in to a communications network like the Web for information, shopping, banking, travel planning, and entertainment; participating in virtual communities; using powerful imaging software to undo reality as we see fit; using multimedia software to learn and play; and engaging in all the other activities that we take for granted today as consumers in the digital age.

Given the pace of change, it's only logical that as technology further evolves and becomes more affordable, we will be doing things with machines that human beings have never done before. In the not-too-distant future, we'll be able to don virtual reality (VR) helmets and sojourn through computer-generated worlds that feel just like the real thing. Our brains will be faked out and our bodies will respond to the stimuli we encounter.

And what kinds of things will we encounter? That depends on the software. One could imagine VR products that enable users to explore, in unique ways, the depths of the seas, the inner workings of the human heart, or the outer reaches of the Milky Way galaxy. One could also imagine virtual time-machine products that enable users to visit the Cretaceous or other prehistoric periods. One can also imagine VR action games that bring violence to new heights or simply soak up hours of free time in mindless pursuits.

Then there are the issues of returning to the mundane world. Will it seem boring? Will people get addicted to realms in which they can get what they want in electronic form, whether it be knowledge, sex, or virtual violence? There may be no consequences to actions taken in virtual reality, but the experiences could have profound effects on the psyches of those who travel inside the machine. And those travelers will be our kids, not today—the equipment available to consumers is still crude—but in the not-distant future. Digital technology has the uncanny potential of making enormous evolutionary leaps whenever there's a perceived market.

We don't have to wait for advanced VR technology to find potential problems wrought by the new technology, however. Children's vulnerability to pedophiles and access to pornography online are making headlines today, and probably will continue to do so long into the future. While both problems have been sensationalized and overstated by the media, they are nonetheless real concerns that require parental awareness, interventions, and rule making.

The bottom line is that from a parenting perspective, computer technology generates new responsibilities. Once you wire into cyberspace, the four walls of your house no longer serve as filters to noxious elements of the outside world. Cyberspace is amoral and boundless; good and bad data travel at the speed of light, and your computer is indifferent as to what those bits mean when they're assembled into images or words.

The solution is not to condemn computer technology, but to recognize that we must take an active role in the way it is used. It's so easy to buy the gear and go about our business, proud that our kids are using a computer, rather than watching TV or getting into trouble on the streets. It's also so easy to simply assume that if our kids are doing something on the computer, they must be learning. That may or may not be true. A young child aimlessly clicking the mouse and listening to cartoon animals go "bleep" isn't having a learning experience. Neither is an older child playing five hours of a "slice 'em and dice 'em" game each day.

The only way to ensure that the computer represents a positive force in your child's life is to get plugged in yourself. You don't need to acquire the equivalent of a Ph.D. in computer science in order to shape your child's experience of digital technology; with a little bit of "mousing" around, you can be computing in no time flat. More important, you can learn to ask your child the right questions so that he or she becomes your teacher, and you can carve a niche for yourself as student and "keyboard copilot." (What a great opportunity for reversing roles and building your child's self-esteem, too!) This isn't to say that you have to hover over every keystroke. But as a plugged-in parent, you'll be in the best position to determine whether the computer is benefiting your child, when to set limits and, most important, how to create bridges from the machine to the real world.

This book is designed to help you ask the right questions and get up to speed. It contains insights based on more than a dozen years of writing computer books, reviewing software for major computing magazines, and testing software in development for software publishers. It also picks up where my previous work with television leaves off. For the past five years, through my books, lectures, and radio appearances, I've tried to help parents teach their children to self-regulate with regard to TV and video games, and to become more media literate.

Now I believe it's time to apply those methodologies to the computer, which is rapidly becoming the hub of activity in many families throughout the country. In 1997, surveys revealed that in some demographic groups, TV viewing was declining in favor of online computing. Expect that trend to continue as the Web evolves into a mainstream source of entertainment. And expect an increasing need to supply what I call *parentware*—the active role we can take in our children's experience of technology. Parentware entails making a commitment to learn about the hardware and software that's making its way into our homes, making informed purchasing decisions, setting standards for acceptable content, serving as a role model, and helping our children make the leap from data to information, from information to knowledge, and from knowledge to meaningful action.

Here's a preview of the kinds of parentware ideas—rules of thumb for healthy digital living, really—that you'll find in the following pages:

## Set Realistic Expectations for the New Technology.

Productivity tool? Education center? Replacement for the TV? New electronic hearth? The computer can play a wide range of roles in your household and in your children's lives. That's why it's important to have a good set of reality-based expectations for PC technology. Chapter 1 looks at some primary reasons people buy PCs, and debunks some common myths with realities about what computers can and can't do for kids.

## Take Stock of What Your Kids Are Doing with the PC.

Do you know what your kids actually do all those hours at the keyboard? Is it educational? Is it healthy? Find out as an involved parent. Chapter 2 encourages you to take an active role and wear three new hats: your family's chief information officer, chief reality officer, and chief traditions officer.

## Seize the Digital Edge.

When used wisely, computers are remarkable tools that can enhance our kids' capabilities and provide a new medium for learning and entertainment. Chapter 3 celebrates what I consider the best of what computers have to offer. The goal of the chapter is to help you create your own best-of list so you can make good decisions for how the computer will be used in your household and how it can live up to its potential as a powerful resource for your children.

## Avoid Potholes on the Cyber Expressway.

As powerful as computers may be, from a parenting perspective the devices can be problematic if used without thought and care. And while the hidden problems shouldn't scare you away from the technology or dampen your family's enjoyment of it, you can't afford to ignore them. As you'll learn in Chapter 4, knowing how computers can have a negative impact on your children will help you devise and deploy effective solutions as you need them.

## Be a Smart Hardware Consumer.

Part of bridging the technology gap involves making good hardware-purchasing decisions. As people flock to the stores to join the home-computing revolution, they often leave with inadequately powered machines or machines filled with worthless components that they'll soon have to upgrade. Chapter 5 explains how to make sound purchasing decisions and how to select a machine that will meet the demands of current software. It will also get you off to the right start and help you save money that you can put toward buying more software—or books, art supplies, and other goodies your kids might enjoy on a rainy day.

## Be an Informed Software Consumer.

Good parentware means taking an active role in choosing the software that will reside on your hard disk. This requires an understanding of what types of programs are most likely to live up to the promises on their boxes. Chapter 6 teaches you how to be your own in-house software reviewer and select programs that will provide the greatest benefit to your children.

## Pick Good Web Sites.

As if it weren't hard enough to choose the best software for your child, you now have to become a Web site reviewer as well! The good news is that it's easy to figure out whether or not a site is appropriate or worth visiting. In Chapter 7, you'll find a set of guidelines for helping you make good

Web choices that ensure your child's time online is well spent.

## Go Beyond the Keyboard; Connect with Your Kids.

As a plugged-in parent, you can greatly extend the shelf life and utility of your software, and you'll make online computing experiences more meaningful. The trick is to pose exciting activities that help your children use the software as tools and resources that complement traditional forms of learning and playing, and that create connections between cyberspace visits and the real world. In Chapter 8, you'll find numerous suggestions for activities that you can create to direct the use of the technology and ensure that it represents a worthwhile and appropriate expenditure of your children's time.

## Be There, Now!

The essence of parentware is involvement; whatever time you have to spare, you can make a contribution to your children's computing experience. And for children exploring the online world, your involvement is essential; you have to be your family's own cybercop. Being involved means setting limits and standards for your kids' computing time. In Chapter 9, you'll find a variety of parentware tips for making computing a positive element of your children's lives, one that contributes to a balanced lifestyle and an appreciation for everyday things. The chapter also stresses the importance of taking actions that help teach your kids to self-regulate with all forms of electronic media.

If all this parentware seems like a lot of work to just bring a computer into your house or to get more use out of what you already own, be assured that it's well worth the effort. You'll minimize potential problems and maximize the chances of your children getting all that they can from today's and tomorrow's electronic offerings.

I'm hopeful that the principles I've provided will apply to emerging digital technologies as well as those in your living room or family room today. As the old saw goes, the best time to make an action plan is before you need one.

Steve Bennett
Cambridge, Mass.
*September 1997*

# The Plugged-In Parent

# Chapter 1

# The Magic Machine

## Setting Realistic Expectations

### *All That Fuss*

"Why do you think computers are important for your kids?" I asked a group of parents assembled for a seminar on kids and technology. Some parents enthusiastically talked about the computer being the wave of the future, and how it would revolutionize their children's education. Others were less sanguine about the devices, but said that they were worried about being left behind in the wake of progress if they didn't purchase the right computer and software, or a computer at all. One parent talked about how technology could bring families together. And another talked about how computing was a major improvement over TV; she described how the family PC finally helped her kids and spouse break their addictions to the tube. Yet another person commented that he had bought a PC for very pragmatic reasons, and that after the novelty wore off, household members simply used the device as they would any appliance. "I don't get what all the fuss is about. Why don't we just use the things and get on with it?" he wanted to know.

The audience's questions covered a broad range of sentiments about computing. A common thread was the passion with which people talked about computers, whether they were speaking out of genuine excitement or the guilt of not providing one for their children. One thing is certain: Many people are confused about just what the new technology will do for their kids, and what sorts of expectations they ought to have. The promises and dreams of living and learning high-tech style are enticing. We all want the best lives for our family members. We want to give our children every possible educational advantage. And we want to provide our kids with the tools and resources that will enable them to confidently enter the job market. Where does the computer fit into all this? Let's return to the talk, and use the audience's concerns and ideas as discussion points.

## Catch the Next Wave of the Future

One parent enthused about computers becoming indispensable for functioning in today's world, and remarked that he didn't want his family to be left behind. This notion is not uncommon; many people believe that if they don't get with it, they'll be relegating themselves and their children to a class of techno-have-nots.

The fact is, we've successfully raised and educated generations of children without computers; children have flourished, led happy and productive adult lives, and engaged in satisfying careers. Buy a computer because you feel it has value, *not* because you feel that there's a virtual gun to your head, or that you'll be like a family without an answering machine.

I believe that if you can afford a computer, there are very compelling reasons to have one in your home sooner rather than later. For you, the computer offers opportunities to save time with word processing, online banking, and a host of productivity boosters. And rhetoric about the wired world aside, the Web is actually turning out to be extremely useful. In just a few short years, it's transformed from being a novelty and free-for-all to a mainstream communication venue. Yes, there are still tens of thousands of silly or useless sites, and sites that are the equivalent of electronic vanity plates. But now that big business has made more of a commitment to the Web, you can find content well worth viewing, such as cutting-edge news with audio and video components; up-to-date listings of events in your home town; and shopping opportunities that make it easier than ever to save time and money. Improved *search engines* make it easier to find good information. And more and more print publications have online counterparts that allow you to search their archives or find valuable additional information and updates.

A year ago, I couldn't imagine reading a newspaper online. While I still enjoy spreading the Sunday edition of *The New York Times* on the living-room floor on a lazy weekend afternoon, I find the daily electronic versions of the *Times* and *The Wall Street Journal* more useful than the print editions. All of the articles contain *links* to related articles that enable me to put events into better context and gain a richer understanding of the topics described. The links to previous articles also make it possible for me to get a historical perspective on an ongoing story.

On a more mundane level, when we want to find out when a specific movie is playing or get a recommendation on something worth seeing, we point our Web browser (the software that allows you to view Web sites) at boston.com, the online version of *The Boston Globe*. We can not only find good movie reviews, but we can search by theater, title, star, type, or time. We can also enter our zip code and find all the nearby theaters playing the film we want to see, then reserve tickets with a credit card. About the only thing the system doesn't do is deliver us to the theater. In our hectic household, we're grateful for anything that saves us precious time; even my skeptical wife, Ruth, admits that this is a good use of technology.

I could go on for pages about the pleasure of shopping for audio CDs at cdnow.com, where I can listen to many of the offerings before buying. Or about the unique experience of buying books online at amazon.com, where I can enjoy services that would be impossible to provide in a conventional retail setting. Among other things, I can read reviews that other customers have posted; then I can offer my own. I can discover all kinds of sites by searching the sites' databases by author, title, or keywords. The prices are good and the delivery excellent, too.

OK, so there are plenty of good reasons for you to add a computer to your life. But what about for your kids? Shopping and checking movie times certainly don't make your list of educational priorities. But there's plenty of good content that awaits them on CD and on the Net.

On the CD-ROM side, you can purchase a variety of multimedia reference tools that have a sound text base and that offer children engaging and compelling presentations. (I recommend World Book and Encarta for general use and for middle schoolers, and Britannica CD or Britannica Online for serious inquiry and older kids.) Paint and drawing programs will enable your kids to express themselves in new ways. A small number of *edutainment* programs can actually serve as useful learning tools. And if you hunt hard enough, you'll find nonviolent games that stimulate creative thinking while providing great entertainment (like the SimCity series, Smart Games, and Oregon Trail III). Excellent keyboarding programs are also available for kids (and for you, too). To be sure, being able to use a word processor is a skill that will serve your children well in school and beyond.

Amidst the junk on the Net you'll find a growing number of sites worthy of your children's time. Museums, educational institutions, and government agencies have significantly beefed up their efforts to provide quality Web sites with expanded information in a lively format. Many public television stations also have excellent sites that supplement their programming. The amount of quality sites and information is getting more impressive each week.

In a sense, all this *is* the wave of the future. But ride it because you believe it will add value to your family members' lives. When you feel pressure to buy, or feel like you're going into the digital age kicking and screaming, you might not do your homework, and you might be inclined to make hasty purchasing decisions. When you defer to a salesperson for all your information, you might purchase something that doesn't serve your family's needs, and that turns out to be an expensive mistake.

## *It's the Future of Education*

A number of parents at the talk said they were motivated to buy a computer because they were convinced that their children would benefit from computing, both at school and, later, in the workplace. Whatever amount of money the computer cost, and whatever amount of time and energy went into learning how to use it, would be worth it, they said. The concern about depriving kids of a powerful educational tool drives folks to the computer superstores in droves. Concern is also generated by the so-called coming crisis in computer literacy. Newspaper and magazine articles bemoan the fact that many schools have antiquated machines that can't even run current-generation software, and that those schools lucky enough to be equipped with adequate PCs make poor, if any, use of them. Many parents are convinced that their kids will be stuck in low-level jobs all their lives if they don't learn how to work the new machines.

I have heard of inspired teachers who use the PC in novel ways, and of schools in which computers are used effectively to convey information and stimulate creativity. Of course, anything that helps children learn is a good thing, and for some kids, compelling software may be just what they need to spark an interest in a new subject. But the notion that computers are *essential* to education and that kids will be at a disadvantage if they aren't productively computing at home is simply untrue.

As technology critic and political scientist Langdon Winner of Rensselaer Polytechnic Institute points out, "Computers have been around in the school for the past fifteen years, and there isn't a shred of evidence that they've made any measurable difference." Echoing Winner's thoughts, Clifford Stoll, a noted computer critic, wrote in *The New York Times* that "computers in classrooms are the filmstrips of the 1990's." As he looked back on his own elementary school experience, he commented: "We loved them [film strips] because we didn't have to think for an hour, teachers loved them because they didn't have to teach, and parents loved them because it showed their schools were high-tech. But no learning happened."

Part of the problem lies with the fact that few teachers know how to use computers productively in their classrooms. This isn't because they're lazy, or incompetent; they're just overworked and underpaid, and they're frequently not given sufficient (if any) training in how to use the machines. Many school administrators are beginning to realize that to make computers a worthwhile component of education, they'll need to hire technology coordinators who can train teachers. This process of locating qualified people and training teachers in-house will not happen overnight, so it's unlikely that your kids will find themselves in a situation anytime soon where they must have computer knowledge to complete homework assignments and projects. Unless the project is specifically for a computer class, the use of the computer for doing an assignment, at least for younger kids, will be optional for the near future, especially given issues regarding equal access to technology.

In short, view the computer as you would any other valuable education resource—as part of a total program that begins at school and continues at home. But don't rely on the computer to fix problems with your child's curriculum. First work hard to find nontechnical solutions to your school system's deficiencies, then apply technology as a sweet enhancement that provides additional depth and richness to the educational process.

## *I Want to Start My Very Young Children at the Computer*

Of all the questions that parents ask, those concerning computers for preschoolers are the most difficult to answer. They're often posed by people who have deep concerns for their children's educational future, but who are guided by too little information. So is it worthwhile to purchase software for preschoolers? On the one hand, little kids love to imitate older sibs and parents, and what could be more fun than playing with a computer?

At the same time, there's no pressing reason to introduce young kids to the computer other than for limited entertainment; as of this writing, there's no compelling evidence that "toddlerware" has a major impact on young children's capabilities or school readiness. In fact, Dr. Susan Haugland of Southeast Missouri State University stopped a research project midstream because she found that constant exposure (an hour per day) to developmentally inappropriate software actually decreased kids' creativity on a number of standard measures. "It would have been unethical to place any more children in front of a monitor to play with programs that would actually be diminishing their capabilities," she said. "Unfortunately, that's what parents do when they're convinced that anything stamped 'ages three to five' will benefit their kids, and that kids who get a jump on computing will somehow gain an advantage."

Haugland did find that developmentally appropriate software gives kids a mild boost in creativity. But she's also quick to point out that it's important to have realistic expectations about any learning technology. "Don't introduce young children to a computer because you think it will give them a head start or for fear that they'll be left behind their peers," she cautions. "Approach the machine with an open mind; if your kids enjoy the computer and it reinforces their newly forming minds, then you've gotten what you can from it."

## *It's a Family Thing to Do*

Pick up an issue of a computing magazine aimed at the home market and you'll likely see a family computing scene that would have made Ozzie and Harriet drool with envy or motivate Norman Rockwell to start a new canvas. If family computing means that people in your household share a computer, teach one another things about programs, and share the output among them, I'm for it.

But there's another aspect that I find troubling—namely, the promise of happiness and togetherness. Look at the ads in the magazines; you'll see . . . happy families! Everyone is having a blast. But you could replace the computer with a new breakfast creation, mouthwash, or shampoo, and you'd see the models radiating the same looks of glee and satisfaction.

The bottom line is that family computing is whatever you make of it. It can be a group of people seated around the screen while one family member serves as the guide. It can be a mother or father co-computing with a child, asking questions and serving as the student. Or it can be individual family members taking turns using the computer to run their favorite programs to do homework, entertain themselves, or manage household finances and communications.

By buying into commercial images of family computing, we set artificial standards, and there are bound to be some disappointments when the computer doesn't become a means of family cohesion. We also reduce the computer to a novelty item—the modern way of spending family time. And we run the risk of diminishing traditional activities that family members have enjoyed doing together for years. Board games, card games, charades, and family antics suddenly become quaint and old-fashioned when compared to the glitzy, fast-paced electronic world.

So look to the computer for what it really can do, and seek family togetherness from the things that really count. You know what to do!

## It Beats TV Hands Down

Many parents are pleased that their kids' computing activities have cut deeply into their TV watching. At first blush, this is a good development. After all, the computer is a mind expander, and the TV is a mind sapper. Even so, our experience with television is pertinent to computing in two ways. First, it's familiar and it provides a backdrop against which we use or abuse the PC. Sometimes we view a specific TV program, and at others we just watch television or surf the channels, looking for anything that captures our interest for a moment. Likewise, sometimes we turn on the computer for a specific purpose, and at other times we boot up to poke around or surf the Net.

When I discuss television issues with parents, I advise them to think about the difference between watching a particular program and simply watching TV or surfing for its own sake. The former can be a constructive effort with the right program; the latter is a poor excuse for something to do.

And just as we can surf the available television networks and cable channels, picking up dribs and drabs to kill time, we also can surf the online services or the Internet, looking for a wave that might catch our attention and reward us for the time we spent.

"But it's educational and interactive," many people say, "while TV is so dumb and passive. Isn't it better for my child?" That all depends on what your child is doing on the computer and how you define interactivity. (See Chapter 6 for a closer look at the concept.) Don't fool yourself by assuming that anything your child does on a computer is in some way educational or mind-expanding; certain computer content can be just as questionable and mind numbing as much of the programming on commercial television. If your child is spending most of the time playing arcade games, there's clearly not much happening from an educational standpoint. The same is true if your toddler is sitting glassy-eyed in front of the screen, aimlessly clicking the mouse on a shape or color, or your youngster is making a cow jump out of a toaster for the fiftieth time as part of a so-called "interactive" storybook.

The fact is, with the right software, the computer *can* provide opportunities for interactive learning and entertainment. But you need to be careful about separating the *potential* for *meaningful* interactivity from the actual state of affairs. While there are some truly excellent software titles to be purchased, far more are hardly an improvement over TV.

The moral? Take stock of what your child is actually doing on the computer before proclaiming that you've progressed beyond television. He or she might be onto something that's truly worthwhile. Or you might find that you're back dealing with another one-eyed monster. If so, act now, before the right to compute in this fashion becomes ingrained. We all know the battles that arise when trying to curb or alter deeply entrenched television-watching habits. Why re-create the situation with our children's inappropriate computing habits? Act now, while we can convey the message that computing, like driving, is a privilege, and not an inalienable right.

## Summary

Your expectations about what the computer can do for your child should be reality based. You should invest in computing gear and software because of what it can actually do for your family. The computer is a uniquely powerful device that can enrich your child's mind and serve your family well, or it can be an extension of the television set. Whether the computer in your house is a dream machine or digital demon depends on how willing you are to actively monitor and moderate its usage.

# Chapter 2

# Computers in the Midst

## Taking Stock and Choosing a Role

### *All That Boots Isn't Gold*

I once had an opportunity to talk to a group of preadolescent boys about their computing activities. "How many hours a day do you spend at the keyboard after school?" I asked. Each boasted that he spent "about four to five hours" per day at his PC for recreational purposes.

"And what do you do with your computers during that time?" I asked, wondering what could sustain the kids' interest for that amount of time. Their answers had a remarkable ring of similarity: They played the latest arcade game, which at the time happened to be Quake. One or two also mentioned that they occasionally went into chat rooms on America Online. And one had access to the Internet through his parents' computer. But he never looked for "swears" or dirty pictures, he assured me.

These kids' parents regarded education as a key priority

and would never consent to their children's watching four to five hours of television per day. So why the permissiveness with the computer? Judging from the parents' reactions when I later demonstrated the games to them, they had no clue as to what their kids were doing at the keyboard.

How could that be, I wondered? It seems that many parents assume that anything their kids do with the computer is worthwhile or educational. After all, the computer—unlike the television set—offers possibilities for learning, flexing creative muscles, and exploring the world. Right?

Yes and no. Some software does indeed offer kids terrific opportunities to learn, flex their creative muscles, and explore the world in unique ways. And many Web sites offer children rich opportunities to learn about science, history, culture, and many other subjects.

But it's also possible for kids to waste an incredible amount of time sitting in front of the monitor with so-called edutainment software that promises to reinforce basic skills, impart knowledge, and enrich young minds, but in fact is little more than a cartoon with a twist. Much of the software on the shelves, particularly programs aimed at very young kids, is of questionable value from a developmental and/or pedagogical point of view. And many learning programs are just drill-and-grill exercises in disguise, offering no insights into why an answer is wrong and how to go about correctly solving a problem.

The bottom line is this: Don't assume that an educational program will live up to the marketing copy on the box. Don't assume that a program or Web site is worthy of your child's time. And don't assume that the computer is adding anything measurable to your child's development. The only way to be certain that your child is getting something worthwhile from the machine is to get closer to the source and see for yourself.

Just how close to the situation are you? Take the following survey and see how you fare:

1. Do you track the amount of time that your child spends on the computer? If so, do you think about it in terms of the percentage of your child's discretionary time? Do you limit your child's time at the computer?

2. Do you research software before you buy it? Read reviews before you buy? Ask your kids' teachers or the parents of your children's friends what software they recommend?

3. Do you allow your child to purchase or install software without an OK or acknowledgment from you?

4. Do you test the software yourself to see what it has to offer? Do you question whether edutainment software is well designed and stimulating? Do you note how various games reward your child?

5. Do you make an effort to determine whether the software fits his or her learning style, whether your child clicks aimlessly at the screen from boredom or lack of direction, or seems to get frustrated because the program is too cryptic or too difficult?

6. Do you talk to your child about why he or she likes a particular program?

7. Do you offer suggestions for creative projects that your child can do on the computer?

8. Do you read the gaming magazines that your child sub-

scribes to or brings home from the newsstand or computer store?
9. Do you select Web sites for your children to visit?
10. Do you have rules for venturing into cyberspace alone?
11. Do you talk about what kind of content is appropriate and what's not?

If you answer no to a lot or most of these, don't feel guilty—you're not alone. Many parents I've informally surveyed are only tangentially involved with their children's computing. This isn't a reflection of their worthiness as caregivers; rather, it reflects a faith in the march of progress and the assumption that since computers are sophisticated devices, kids will do sophisticated things with them. But as we saw in the beginning of this chapter, that's often not the case.

## Why Bother?

I'm sometimes accused of being Polyannaish about my concerns for parental involvement with computing. But in fact, we are heading into uncharted territory. We have no experience raising a generation of kids who have access to immense power for manipulating reality. We don't know what spending vast amounts of time in virtual realms and machine-generated simulations will do to kids in terms of their appreciation of action and consequences in the real world. Even the experts on computers and society are at odds about the impact of these developments.

If you read the writings and listen to the comments of digital evangelists, you'll learn that computers and related technologies will be central to our future—a very rosy future at that. Kids in the digital era will learn faster than any prior generation, be able to do things that no other generation can do, and have unparalleled access to information through global communication networks.

As Nicholas Negroponte, the high-profile director of MIT's famous Media Lab, asserts in his book, *On Being Digital,* "My optimism comes from the empowering nature of being digital. The access, the mobility, and the ability to effect change are what will make the future so different from the present. The information superhighway may be mostly hype today, but it is an understatement about tomorrow. As children appropriate a global information resource, and as they discover that only adults need learner's permits, we are bound to find new hope and dignity in places where very little existed before."

On the other hand, if you read the writings and listen to the warnings of technocritics, you'll get the impression that the road to hell is paved with silicon. You'll learn that humanity itself is at stake if we let digital technology make further incursions into our lives, or if we venture much deeper into cyberspace. John Slouka, of the University of California, San Diego, for example, writes that we "stand on the threshold of turning life itself into computer code, of transforming the experience of living in the physical world—every sensation, every detail—into a product for our consumption. . . . Computer simulations may soon be so pervasive (and so realistic) that life itself will require some mark of authenticity. Reality, in other words, may one day come with an asterisk."

I agree with elements of both arguments; while digital

technology can serve as a marvelous tool for boosting productivity, organizing information, facilitating communication, and providing new outlets for creativity, it can indeed rob us of our humanity and send us careening into uncharted territory.

Unfortunately, we don't have the luxury of sitting around and debating whether or not the technology is for the good or bad of our species. It's here now, and we need to find ways of drawing on its best aspects and avoiding its worst. For so many kids, the computer is already a commonplace medium for entertainment, learning, and communication. And in the year 2000, according to a study by Forrester Research, a major research company that tracks the computer industry, 27 percent of eighteen-year-olds will have grown up with PCs in their households.

The kids of the PC generation will be as comfortable expressing themselves via computer as the previous generation was with pens, pencils, crayons, and markers. Word processing will be second nature to them. They'll know how to communicate via multimedia presentations. They'll be perfectly at home with e-mail and with exploring the world through online services and the World Wide Web. And they'll expect instant access to information of all sorts through online databases, CD-ROMs, and *hybrid* CDs updated by links to Web sites. In short, they'll be the first wired generation to walk the planet. Technology will give them a new set of tools to use, but they're going to need a lot of coaching to put those tools to good use.

And that's where you come in. You may not be a professional educator, but as a parent, you're the best expert in your child's development. And your involvement can only be a positive force in making technology a beneficial force in your child's life.

## *A New Role for You: The Family CIO*

You may consider yourself to be your family's president or chairperson of the board, but in the digital age, you'll need to don the hat of chief information officer as well. That's because your kids, unlike any children before them, will be privy to a wealth of electronic information that hitherto could only be afforded by corporations and institutions. Information about everything under the sun practically pours out of CD-ROMs and your Web-connected modem.

On the one hand, this is very exciting. We all like the idea of having oodles of information on tap. On the other, the info flood poses new challenges and requires new skills. With so much information at our children's fingertips, we'll need to teach them how to make good editorial judgments about what's wheat and what's chaff. That requires new skills on our part, and an awareness that it's easy to get swept away in a sea of raw data. So it's worth your while to get familiar with Web search engines (see Chapter 7) and with showing your kids how to home in on the information they need.

The good news is that it's fun. Try finding some information about a topic of interest to you, then make a game of it with your kids. That's exactly how I helped my ten-year-old, Noah, begin to think of the computer as a tool that could help him with his homework and answer his questions about the way things of the world work. We started off using

Microsoft's Encarta and IBM's World Book Encyclopedia as our sources. The first "assignment" I gave Noah was based on a story that he and I had been making up about creatures who live on the sun. I suggested that he find some information about the sun, so our story would be more realistic (insofar as you can get realistic about guys from space visiting the sun). I showed him how to find topics in the two multimedia encyclopedias, and he eagerly began collecting facts for our story (such as the sun's interior temperature of twenty-nine million degrees Fahrenheit, and the constitution of the sun's corona).

Over the next weeks, we moved on to other topics that I knew would pique his curiosity, such as the Loch Ness Monster and Bigfoot. For each topic he eagerly dove into the CD and came back with a report containing facts and figures.

Since then, we expanded our info-searching game to the Web. We search together, but Noah drives. I'm there as a coach to advise him on what's likely to be junk and what's worth looking at. I'm confident that as he gets older, he'll be able to find just about any type of information he needs quickly and efficiently, which means he'll have more time to think and to synthesize data from a number of sources.

Try it yourself. Create assignments that strike a responsive chord with your kids. You know their interests and what will turn them into information hounds. The exercise not only is a good way for you to familiarize yourself with the tools, but also will make you feel involved with an important and very tangible aspect of your kids' computing experience.

There's one caveat in all of this: We need to realize that the very tools our children use to search for information can become blinders. This became apparent to me a few years ago when I signed up for a trial subscription to an electronic version of *The Wall Street Journal*. The "Personal *Journal*" was not only cheaper than buying the real thing, but I would only receive information in the categories I wanted (that's the "personal" part). So I chose topics such as technology, small business, and marketing trends. After several days of downloading the Personal *Journal*, I went back to buying the paper each morning.

Initially, I thought that my problem with the electronic paper was that I missed the feel of the real thing as well as the ritual of saying hello to my neighbors and local shopkeepers as I walked to the newsstand. Then it dawned on me that my discomfort with the electronic newspaper was more subtle; by selecting a limited number of information categories, I had lost the opportunity for serendipitous discovery. In fact, the more I thought about it, the more I realized that some of the most interesting stories I'd read came about through nonpurposeful skimming.

There are certainly times when the ability to zero in on a topic is desirable. But it's always rewarding to seize an opportunity to browse and enjoy what you find along the way. Many people who grew up using print encyclopedias for homework discovered this firsthand; they learned as much from browsing the cross-referenced volumes as they did from the original assignment. I certainly did, and even today enjoy getting sidetracked when I use encyclopedias and other resources (print and electronic) to find information. (I've also resubscribed to *The Wall Street Journal* online, now that the full paper is available. I can search for specifics or skim through the various sections in search of tidbits that will be of use to me.)

Some publishers of electronic encyclopedias recognize the value of browsing and include a "random" button that plucks a topic from the database and displays it for casual reading. This is a welcome addition. If you have one, make a game of the function. Perhaps suggest that once or twice a week your son or daughter surprise everyone with a fact, figure, or concept learned from a random walk through a CD. (If the encyclopedia doesn't have a random browse function, your kids can move the cursor to a list of topics or articles and just click when the spirit strikes.)

However you do it, encourage your children to browse aimlessly, as well as purposefully, to quickly locate information. You'll be giving them a gift far more valuable than the computer and all the software you've provided.

## CRO *(Chief Reality Officer)*

A common assumption is that electronic communication will create a new *global village* that brings people across the world closer together than ever before. That's an old concept that media visionary Marshall McLuhan talked about in the sixties, well before the advent of personal computers and the Web. And in some ways, there's a lot of truth to it. After all, we can communicate with people many thousands of miles away via e-mail and join them in newsgroups and forums. And as technology progresses, I have no doubt that audiomail and videomail will become standard communication fare; both are already here today, though in simple form. They will make it possible for people to truly collaborate on projects in ways unheard of now. The faceless nature of the Net will disappear.

At the same time, let's not fool ourselves into believing that technology by itself will break down social and economic barriers and lead to a true electronic global village. If *global* simply means *geographic,* then the promise is certainly fulfilled; you can communicate electronically with anyone, anywhere on the planet. But if global has a social dimension, then the situation changes considerably. For when we communicate electronically we largely talk to mirrors; that is, we talk to people who are fortunate enough to have access to computers, just as we do. Such folks, of course, represent a tiny percentage of the people in the world. So while the idea of shrinking the globe may sound good theoretically and feel good politically, the reality is that the global village consists of a small minority of haves—the rest of the world has little prospect for joining the digital dialogue in the foreseeable future.

This is important for your kids to know, especially those approaching or in their teen years, when they may well develop a social conscience, and start thinking about solving world problems like hunger and poverty. When they see ads showing people of various cultures typing on laptops in the fields and marketplace, or ads showing one child e-mailing another child in a faraway country, they need to understand that they're watching scenes that aren't representative of the majority of the world's population. They also need to understand that computers and communication networks are good tools, but it will take real work to solve real world problems.

## *CTO (Chief Traditions Officer)*

Many arguments about the electronic age are framed as either-or propositions. That is, we either accept new technologies or go back to the Pre-Digital Age. As I'll stress throughout this book, there's a mid path, one that blends technology and tradition. If your kids are into virtual museum tours, make an extra effort to take actual museum tours. Ditto for libraries and parks and other places we can visit on the Web and still take advantage of in the real world.

So much depends on how we present the computer to our kids—whether we put it on a pedestal or introduce it as a powerful, yet pedestrian, appliance. In households that take the appliance approach, the computer becomes just another tool. I call this the "Number 2 pencil" model: We have paper, we have crayons, we have pencils and, by the way, we also have the computer.

If you put the computer in its place, you have the best chance of enjoying the proven benefits of traditional forms of learning and exploring the world. And there's an indisputable benefit to balancing screen time with life time so that the former doesn't obliterate activities, sports, hobbies, and what little family time is left today. In some households, the computer has become a virtual hideout for family members and an impediment to activities that have long kept children's bodies fit and their minds sharp. By reducing the computer to just another thing in the house, you make it easier to initiate and maintain the balancing act.

# *Summary*

We have many choices to make regarding technology in our homes, and not just about what kind of software we buy and what our kids can do online. We can purchase devices or software that restricts television, phone, and computer use. Do we opt for these little boxes and programs or help our kids self-regulate and learn valuable lessons? The latter option is surely better, but it takes more work and commitment. To the extent that you're willing to become a plugged-in parent, you can pluck the best of what the digital age has to offer and bring it into your household in a way that enriches your children's lives.

# Chapter 3

# The Digital Edge

## Making Technology Work for Your Kids

### *Thinkin' About Computing*

"What's this?" my ten-year-old son, Noah, asked as he held up a review copy of Edmark's Strategy Games of the World CD-ROM.

"It's a program that teaches you about three old games," I answered. "Want to check it out and tell me if you think I should write about it?"

Noah agreed, and we installed the software in our family playroom. A few minutes later, I heard the narrator on the disk explaining the history and rules of Nine Men's Morris, a deceptively simple game in which players take turns placing shells on a grooved board, then try to eliminate their opponents' shells by aligning their own in mills (three shells in a row). I then heard the disk's strategy coach guiding Noah through a few games. After several rounds, Noah popped his head into my office and asked, "Dad, can we buy a real one?"

As it happened, our local game store stocked a nice wooden Nine Men's Morris board that included colored marbles as playing pieces—all for $9.95. The game became an instant hit with everyone in the family, and we became quite obsessed with it for several weeks. Although we played with the board and marbles, Noah continued to consult the CD for advanced strategic and tactical tips. And his game showed it. My low-tech wife, Ruth, also got dramatically better; perhaps she was hitting the keyboard at night. Computers have a way of occasionally impressing even the most avowed Luddite.

Our experience with Strategy Games of the World was gratifying for several reasons. First, it introduced us to a wonderful game, one that we probably wouldn't have discovered on our own. Second, it provided superb instruction suited for children and adults alike—that, in itself, is a remarkable achievement. Finally, it demonstrated how high-tech approaches to learning and playing can nicely integrate with low-tech/no-tech fun and games—something important to us. In short, the computer proved to be a very useful adjunct to our closetful of games and puzzles.

For other people, the computer's ability to serve up recipes from a cooking CD, data from a multimedia encyclopedia, or breaking news from a Web site is what makes it today's dream machine. I could describe the dream-machine aspect of computers by discussing specific programs in a variety of genres. But that's what the computer magazines are for; you'll find current reviews of the latest offerings. Here, I want to present a more generic way of considering what computers can do for us and our kids. (In Chapter 6 I'll provide a framework for building a software library for your kids.)

## *Sharpening Minds Through "What-If" Thinking*

We usually think of computers in the context of specific tasks. And we relate specific tasks to categories of software. For example:

- A word processor is a tool for creating documents on screen or paper.
- A spreadsheet is used to manipulate numbers.
- A paint or drawing program is used to create electronic art.
- A photo-editing program allows us to fix, alter, and prepare digital images.
- A desktop publishing program allows us to create sophisticated layouts.

Now think about the same programs as what-if tools that enable us to test various scenarios onscreen without going through the laborious task of creating physical representations by hand:

- A word processor enables us to easily do what-if thinking in terms of composition. (For example, "What if this thought precedes this one, or vice versa?")
- A spreadsheet enables us to test various scenarios without

creating numerous ledger sheets. ("What if we earn 10 percent more next year—how much closer will that bring us to our college savings goals?")

- A paint program allows us to experiment with lines, colors, and shapes. ("What if I add this brush stroke or change this tint?")
- A photo-editing program allows us to experiment with composition, lighting, color, and special effects. ("What if we crop the picture this way and soften the image a bit?")
- A desktop publishing program allows us to test various layout presentations, and introduce or subtract graphic elements. ("What if this picture in our newsletter goes here and that column of text goes there?")

In other words, the software has more than just a utilitarian function of helping us accomplish tasks more efficiently; it can help us solve problems more effectively and express our thoughts in new and creative ways. This is more than a matter of definition or a philosophical exercise; framing the computer as a unique what-if tool opens the door for creative thinking and the freedom to experiment.

Consider word processing. These days, word processing is probably the most ubiquitous application among computer users, and it's hard for many people to imagine ever again writing more than a couple of pages by hand or by typewriter. (I can't.) You can look at a word processor as a means of creating documents, or as an invitation to experiment with form and structure.

Beyond productivity software, well-designed packages for kids elevate what-if thinking to a high art. For instance, one of the most popular games in software history is the Sim series of games, in which players try to optimally balance needs and resources in various contexts, such as a city or rainforest. In doing so, they hone their reasoning skills and can extend their what-if thinking to problems in the real world.

Game creator and cofounder of Maxis Software Will Wright puts it this way: "Kids are natural problem solvers. They get a terrific thrill from trying alternatives and building models. They like to feel like experts, too, when they find a working solution." Wright also notes that simulation and creativity games give kids an important opportunity to make decisions and appreciate the consequences of their choices—all within a safe context.

Parents, Wright believes, can build on that decision-making experience to talk about solving problems in the real world. "Software can provide a new frame of reference for interacting with your child," he says. Wright and his nine-year-old daughter, Cassidy, constantly draw on their experience with the Sim products. "We talk a lot about the future," he says, "imagining what the world could be like if certain things were to happen. What-if stuff that kids love to discuss, such as life on other planets, the return of the dinosaurs, magic cures, and so on."

Wright also believes that simulation games are particularly good for teaching kids to be patient. "There's no instant gratification when you play a game like SimTown," he says. "You have to do things in trial-and-error fashion, just like in real life." He sees evidence of his daughter's growing level of patience all the time. When he and Cassidy go fossil hunting, for example, they might come up empty-handed after an hour. Rather than getting frustrated, Cassidy will eagerly participate in a dialogue about what went wrong. Perhaps they're in the wrong place, maybe they're looking at the wrong kind of rock, etc. "What's most important to me is that she'll be thinking and analyzing," Wright says, both as a successful software developer and proud father.

Even when the what-if potential isn't an integral part of a program, most software offers opportunities for you to ask good what-if questions that encourage experimentation. For example: "What if you choose this font instead of that one?" "What if you mix these two colors together instead of those two (and use the *Undo* function)?" "What if you move this paragraph here?" "What if you place this photo here?" And so on—the possibilities are limited only by your own imagination!

## *Novel Outlets for Expressing Creativity*

The digital revolution has brought with it a variety of exciting new ways for children and adults to focus on creative pursuits. Many teachers, for example, encourage their young students to write stories with a word processor even when they're learning to improve their penmanship and write longhand. The word processor can provide a welcome break from (although not a replacement for) the arduous task of learning the fundamentals of handwriting, allowing children to focus on developing story plots and characters, and to express their thoughts and feelings. (You don't have to wait for your child's teacher to suggest this kind of story writing; assign your own stories and make a tradition of reading them aloud.)

Some software publishers have upped the creativity ante by offering word-processing products that allow children to create *electronic books* containing text, pictures, sounds, and even simple movies. These can produce striking multimedia books that add new dimensions to story making and storytelling. Children who grow up using these kinds of writing tools will be capable of presenting information in new and exciting ways. With the right guidance, they'll also become experts at using a medium in which the traditional lines between text, graphics, and audio elements blur and fade. Will this development turn every child into a potential computer artist? Probably not. But the ability to intertwine traditionally distinct media will in turn help children discover hidden strengths, interests, and talents that might otherwise go unnoticed.

Other types of software, such as paint and drawing programs, enable kids to manipulate color and space in ways simply not possible with conventional media. Again, the dream-machine aspect lies not in the ability of the computer to mimic what your kids traditionally do with paper, pencil, markers, brushes, and pigments, but in the incredible capacity of the software to manipulate textures, space, and color in new ways. With proper encouragement and guidance, children can come to regard the computer as a special creativity tool that complements other available media.

## Means for Stimulating a New Visual Awareness

The advent of graphics software and printers capable of generating a variety of fonts, rules, and sundry graphic elements has made form an essential aspect of creating content. In other words, the visual presentation becomes tightly entwined with the message. While this is a double-edged sword (it's easier than ever to create documents that violate the most basic tenets of graphic design and typography), PCs and laser printers have made people far more aware of the role of type and layout in communication.

Even children can appreciate the interconnections between form and function. "I always typed my homework assignments," recalls Kristen Buck, "then one day I started playing with fonts. I was amazed that the kind of font and the size really changed how the words felt when I read them." Kristen, who was fourteen years old when I interviewed her, applied that lesson when her English teacher made several poetry assignments. For one assignment she wrote a poem about a young person who "stole a car and almost got caught." She then used typography to enhance the imagery. For example, most of the poem was written in "jumbo letters" to express a sense of rebelliousness. But when the main character was running away, Kristen used small, condensed letters to convey a sense of motion. At another point in the poem, people were "waiting for a long time," so she increased the intraletter and intraword spacing until she felt that the words and type meshed, and the poem took on new meaning.

Try it yourself; ask your own children to write several sentences on the computer—some happy, some neutral, and some sad—and then to experiment with different typefaces. What effects on the communication do your kids report? You can do the same kind of experiments with white space, shaded areas, italics, bold type, rules, and other elements, too. You'll be amazed at how altering graphic details can change the message, and how quickly you and your kids will be able to pick up on the subtle relationship between form and content. Chapter 8 presents a variety of other visual-awareness activities.

## *Tools for Developing Collaborative Projects*

These days, we hear a lot about how the Web will bring together students in diverse communities around the world. "Aha, pen pals," you're probably thinking. If so, you're not alone; many teachers have jumped on the bandwagon. But, as many teachers have discovered, pen pal projects aren't a particularly good use of the computer. According to psychologist James A. Levin of the University of Illinois (as cited in *The Computing Teacher Journal*), children often participate enthusiastically at first, e-mailing messages to their counterparts in distant classrooms, but excitement soon wanes. Prospective pen pals may take a long time to respond, and the long and unpredictable wait often frustrates the once-eager letter writers. Sometimes responses are not forthcoming, and some students receive letters while others don't. The inequity can be difficult for kids. As the program continues, responses often become less frequent, and even the "lucky" kids soon find themselves feeling snubbed.

End of the dream machine as the great communication facilitator? No, just a false start. You might look at what Levin calls the Noon Observation Project as the kind of project that does a better job of harnessing the usefulness of the Internet by enabling students to work together even though they're separated by long distances. In this project (a modern-day variation of a famous experiment first performed by the ancient Greek geographer, Eratosthenes, who measured the shadow of a stick to determine the North-South circumference of the earth), scores of trigonometry classes around the country followed a protocol to measure noon shadows, then shared their results via the Internet. Classes communicated by e-mail and arranged to transmit their data at a certain day and time. With the geographically diverse data, the students in the various schools were able to independently make highly accurate calculations of the earth's circumference. This collaborative project would have been extremely difficult without the Internet, which made it possible for the students to communicate data quickly and without the administrative headaches of trafficking paper or voice communications.

## *A Catalyst for Encouraging Negotiation and Sharing*

Most households boast fewer computers than users, which means someone often wants to supplant another person at the keyboard. This can be grounds for trouble, and many families report that their home PCs have become triggers for internecine squabbling that they haven't seen since the early days of sibling rivalry.

Instead, family members can use the computer as a vehicle for practicing their negotiating skills. They may talk about their practical needs for the computer—for example, a parent may want to use a money-management program to balance checking accounts, a high schooler may want to search the World Wide Web to do research for a paper, and a younger child may want to use a computer game.

If you have a good process in place for negotiating and making democratic decisions, it will be easy to create a set of guidelines for using the machine. If not, the new computer might serve as a catalyst for putting such a process in place.

The bottom line is that once we have computers, the devices have a tendency to become very entwined in our daily life. So it will become increasingly important for family members to learn the arts of negotiating, reasoning, and listening to reconcile one another's technological wants and needs. In a sense, the home PC creates an additional forum for establishing new family dynamics that can ultimately help children (and adults) become more successful social beings.

## *The Great Motivator*

Technology instills a sense of wonder in children and can issue them passports to worlds they didn't even know existed. It might also inspire a passion in kids for wanting to learn more about a subject. For example, a child who uses a CD to learn about the ocean may develop a passion for marine biology. The computer beckons to kids, and encourages them to enter all of the worlds that are available to them. As a result, a child will learn that he or she doesn't have to be just a member of the class, or a citizen of a town, city, state, or country. Technology gives kids permission to go to any destination reachable online or any environment created in a quality program.

But even if your child doesn't take a literal dive into the ocean after getting excited about the underwater world through a compelling software program, he or she still stands to benefit. Some teachers and parents report that well-designed CD-ROMs and Web sites often get kids interested enough about subjects so that they want to learn more. Even children who traditionally spurn books have been known to eagerly head to the computer to play with a great piece of software to do research. As these teachers and parents point out, it's not unusual to see otherwise-reluctant students latch onto new interests, whether dinosaurs, art, or wildlife, and move from CD-ROMs on the topics to magazines, museum trips, and other fact-finding missions. Some newly motivated information seekers even compile unsolicited extra-credit reports for school. Kids who have histories of doing well in school similarly thrive when given access to well-designed CDs; the depth and breadth of information (a single CD-ROM can contain tens of thousands of pages, images, and sounds) provide a basis for mastery of a wide variety of subjects for independent learners.

## *Empowerment for Children*

For the first time in history, kids are in a position to leapfrog ahead of their parents. Kids understand computers intuitively and can acquire knowledge easily, which creates a wonderful opportunity for them to become essential guides for parents who are unfamiliar with computers and have, in effect, entered a foreign territory with a strange new language. With this new mentoring role for children comes unprecedented power. According to family therapist Carleton Kendrick, "The home computer offers an opportunity for a child to say, with all good grace, 'Mother, father, or older brother or sister, I have something that I can teach you that has value.' " Kendrick believes that this "gives kids an exponentially greater chance to gain respect and engage parents at a peer level. For what he or she is really saying is that 'I have something I'm learning about in school or on my own, and if you want to be competent in this world we're living in, you're going to need to learn it, too.' " When parents and children can challenge each other with a safety cushion of mutual respect and love, Kendrick says, there is a greater probability that the child will evolve as an independent, responsible individual with a strong sense of self-esteem— which is every parent's desire.

Empowerment also involves the children's ability to break free of convention and create worlds of their own in which the line between the actual and the possible disappears. When computer tools are presented appropriately, kids' naïveté about what supposedly can't be done or can't exist doesn't hold them back from fearlessly experimenting with the electronic resources at their fingertips. They can *morph* (photographically transform) people into cats, create the appearance of textures never experienced in real life, and colors and shades they've never seen before. Such opportunities are not only excellent means for expressing creativity, but they empower children to become the architects of a special landscape of their own making. And they can do so because the computer is completely nonjudgmental. Technology provides kids with a window into a world in which anything they imagine is possible. As Kendrick puts it, "When children use computers to sever the ties that bind them to adults' imaginations, then they begin to see that the emperor (or the universal adult) has no clothes because they can see it and do it on the computer."

Finally, for many kids, online computing can be a great equalizer. When children log on, they don't have to state their height, weight, muscle or dress size. In virtual space, there are no points for running fast, pressing heavy weights, looking pretty, hitting home runs, or being thinner. Instead, kids enter the world of technology as they are. Says Kendrick, "This frees them at all developmental stages from the superficial posturing they usually need to gain respect from their peers and adults. In short, technology empowers them to go beyond the social artifacts associated with their physical beings, and feel good about themselves as intelligent and creative individuals with knowledge they can contribute and feelings they can share."

# *Summary*

Yes, the computer does have a tremendous dream-machine potential. But as parents and teachers, we need to ensure that the machine doesn't become an end, rather than a means, to higher learning, creativity, and connections to others. Remember, it is the interaction between informed adults and curious students that gives meaning to the technology; the dream machine can only become a reality if we approach the computer with full presence of mind, consciousness, and the spirit of guidance.

## Chapter 4

# Speed Traps and Power Plays

## Avoiding Hidden Potholes on the Cyber Expressway

### *Of Virtual Fish and Real Kids*

Nineteen ninety-six was not a very good year for my family's aquarium; a spate of viral and bacterial infections, a lethal pH imbalance, and an early-morning acrobatic act cost us our favorite stock. We lost Captain Kid (a swordtail molly), Highway (a blue-fin tetra), Fish One (a balloon molly), and Fish Two (a black-tailed molly). All of our departed aquatic friends reside at the far edge of the garden, marked by special stones or assemblages of twigs.

Ah, but wouldn't it be so much easier for everyone if we just gave away the remaining fish, disconnected the aerator and filter, drained the tank, and booted up Aquazone, a program that one mail-order catalog describes as "The world's first 'virtual' pet software . . . lets you create, customize, and maintain tropical fish aquariums. . . . Aquazone re-creates the natural beauty of real tropical fish *without all the work* [emphasis added]." The description includes a rave plug from *Wired* magazine that says, "A virtual aquarium so real that the only thing missing is the smell." Wow—an aquarium with no muss or fuss! No real water to mess up your floor. No excretions to filter. No smelly algae to scrape. Best of all, when the fish die, you don't have to dig up the gardenias to bury them.

As mesmerizing as Aquazone may be, there's nothing like the soothing vibrations of a real aerator stone, the calming sound of real bubbles breaking through the water's surface, and the suspense of watching real fish make their unpredictable moves and maneuvers. Then, too, the experience of caring for and losing fish has helped our children appreciate the delicacy of life and the permanence of death, and the fact that we go on doing and caring despite the events taking place in the tank. For kids who haven't been desensitized to suffering and death through television and videos, the lessons of the fish tank are powerful stuff.

Now, I don't think there's any danger of my kids or any other children confusing the fish on the computer screen with the real thing. And the Aquazone program is harmless and entertaining. What's troubling, though, is the underlying notion that you can enjoy the same thrills of a real aquarium without the negatives—the work (if you count that a negative), the odors, the ongoing expenses, and so on. It's just too easy. And this notion exemplifies a fundamental problem with concepts such as virtual reality: You engage in a realm with no real consequences. (If things get too messy, reboot.)

"So what's the big deal?" you might ask. "It's just a game that has no effect on real life."

But, in fact, the electronic media that we and our kids use every day shape our behaviors and perceptions in many subtle ways that extend far beyond the actual viewing sessions. Television is the most obvious example; so much of what children learn about making their way through the world originates with the tube. Though the vast majority of kids won't commit violent crimes as a result of watching violent shows, few kids are completely unaffected by messages about conflict resolution, the disposability of certain groups of people, sexuality, consumerism, the ideal body type, and the like.

Computers can also affect children and adults in surprising ways. For instance, they can easily distort our sense of time and diminish our tolerance for things that don't happen on demand. They can fool us into believing that anything invented more than six months ago is virtually obsolete and nearly worthless. And they can cause us to devalue people we meet online, believing they're somehow worthy of less respect than those we meet face-to-face. This chapter explores a variety of subtle problems that won't likely make the headlines, as glitzy issues like cyberporn will, but nonetheless can have a profound influence on the lives of our children.

## *Hooked on Speed*

Pick up a computer magazine and browse through the ads. You'll quickly see a common theme: speed. You're likely to see images comparing things that plod to things that zoom along—a bicycle to a rocket, or a turtle to a thoroughbred.

You'll see people with their hair blowing straight back or their faces distorted because they're moving so fast. You'll see lots of jet planes, rockets, race cars, and other symbols of speed. Then flip through the editorial pages and articles, and you'll find countless references to *blazing speed, blistering speed, speed demons,* and the like.

Part of the need for speed is technical. To handle complex software and provide a sustained viewing experience on par with television or motion pictures, computers require an immense amount of power. Today's software is also becoming more and more processor hungry, so the speed of the computer is a definite consideration if you want to run many current programs. But there's far more to the allure of speed than meeting technical requirements. There's an implicit assumption that faster is better. Why? Presumably because we'll "work smarter, not harder" (another common industry slogan). Or perhaps it's simply because our dependence on computers has raised *efficiency* to the status of a modern religion.

Maybe we're even rewiring our brains; two seconds can seem like an eternity when you're in the fast lane of computing. I confess that my own sense of time has become warped as a result of extensive computer usage. *Wait* has become a four-letter word, and the hourglass a loathsome image (the hourglass indicates that the computer is *processing,* and in many cases, it means you can't do anything except twiddle your thumbs until it finishes).

The sense of urgency that starts at the keyboard spills over into other aspects of our and our children's lives. It's no wonder that kids steeped in a culture that reveres speed have so little tolerance for things that don't happen instantly.

Fortunately, one of the goals of parenting is to teach patience and curb children's need of instant gratification. As child psychiatrist Dr. David Hawkins points out: "More and more kids are clearly moving too fast through life. Their patience span is frighteningly short. Computers can contribute to that sense of *gimme now* because they do give it now. Parents need to help kids realize that the real world doesn't mimic the world of the computer. As computers and electronic toys and games become a more standard part of kids' lives, the imperative will be on every parent to counterbalance the expectation that everything happens when you will it. Life isn't just a menu with options that you choose with your mouse and, presto, you have it in front of you. Patience really is a virtue for kids, and it's something that needs to be cultivated at each stage of development."

## *Power to the User*

Next to speed, *power* is the predominant theme in the computer world. Peruse the computer magazines and you'll see the term frequently used in ads and articles. Terms like *power user* and *power tools* abound, as do images of natural forces and machines that connote immense strength.

The computer is also frequently described as an enabling and empowering technology. In many ways, computers do extend our reach. With a little help from built-in software wizards (step-by-step helpers), even the most graphically unsophisticated user can create remarkable visual works and stunning layouts. People who can't balance their checkbooks can build complex spreadsheets. Students with no formal library-science skills can pinpoint a wealth of resources from Web sites around the world. The list could go on.

But there's another aspect of computing power that brings out the worst in human nature. We see it all too often with another technology, the automobile. We've all seen people who are otherwise perfectly civil transform into monsters when they sit behind the wheel of a car. The gas pedal becomes an extension of their feet, and the car itself becomes an extension of their bodies, fueled by anger. They honk and make obscene gestures at those who don't have the good sense to keep up their pace or get out of their way. They curse and shout in ways that they'd never find appropriate at home or at work. And God help any driver in front of them who waits more than a nanosecond after the light turns green.

A similar Jekyll-and-Hyde transformation takes place when some people venture onto the information highway. The keyboard becomes an extension of their fingers, and the computer, with its connection into cyberspace, an extension of their body. But unlike obnoxious drivers, these "empowered" individuals have no faces or vehicles that can be remembered, no license plates that can be easily traced and reported. In cyberspace, you're anonymous; in most online arenas, people see only your *handle* (an electronic pseudonym); in virtual-reality contexts, they see only your *avatar* (a graphic image that you maneuver through a spatial environment and use to communicate with other people's avatars on the screen).

The combination of power and anonymity leads to a range of exchanges that would be unimaginable in real life, even to the people who commit them. Explicit sexual harassment, for example, is prevalent throughout cyberspace. People with feminine names online are often asked first about their various body parts and their sexual preferences. No wonder so many women adopt names that don't reveal their gender. Others who feel empowered by online computing engage in rampant flaming, an abusive form of communication in which one person lashes out and browbeats another because of his or her statements or comments.

Nothing better illustrates this problem than the *intergenerational wars* that have taken place in cyberspace, in which twenty- and young thirtysomethings unabashedly—though anonymously—have fired off posts like:

POST: You old folks are sapping the life out of today's generation. I am paying mucho dollars into SS, and I will probably never get any of it back. Do you think you are somehow owed more money because you faught in a war? Well, you are dead wrong. Service to this country is a duty, and not something you should expect a monetary return on. This is no welfare state. Go to some commie country for handouts.

A RESPONSE: Don't confuse Social Security with Veterans Benefits. By the way when did you serve your country in the armed forces?

ANOTHER RESPONSE: "Faught" is spelled "Fought." Stop trying to keep up with everyone else financially, contribute your share like the rest of us did, and unless you've fought in a war NEVER treat it lightly!

I suspect that the people posting these messages would be at least civil to older folks on the street, and that it's highly unlikely they'd collar seniors and begin screaming at them for "siphoning off the social security system"—old age still commands a modicum of respect in our society. In effect, though, the electronic mask allows people to metaphorically grab anyone else by their virtual lapels and rattle their teeth for whatever reasons they deem worthy. One could argue that the technology gives seniors, and everyone else in cyberspace, an opportunity to play on a level field. How sad, though, if anonymity is the only way some people feel safe enough to approach one another or express their feelings.

Real communication is about honesty, not about cowardly guerrilla attacks from the vantage point of a faceless and nameless virtual world. Conveying this idea is a major challenge for parents. It's so easy for young and old people alike to feel strong and brave when no one can see them. And it's equally easy to forget that behind every nickname, pseudonym, or avatar there's a human being with real feelings.

## Dollar for Dollar: Of Holes in Our Wallets and Holes in Our Heads

My father once remarked that sending me to college was like losing a clotting factor in his checkbook. Some twenty-three years later, he made the same comment about the ongoing costs of his computer, noting that the initial $2,200 he'd ponied up for the machine was just the start, once he got a taste of all the software he'd like to own. He's pretty sure my college education was worth it, but it took him a while to feel the same about the computer acquisition. (He's now become part of the "wired" senior set.)

As my father discovered, computers have an insatiable appetite for new content, and temporary relief usually comes in the form of $29, $39, and $49 bites (somewhat higher for business software programs). It's easy to forget that the real expenses begin after you buy the computer, especially if you bought a home computer with all kinds of bundled software and assumed that you got everything you and your kids would need. It's also easy to fall into the "if it's related to the computer, it must be good" trap, and sanction purchases that are grossly out of whack with other items in your household budget.

Nothing brought this home to me better than an experience I had riding the subway from Boston to Harvard Square one afternoon. Three kids sitting across from me, probably seventh or eighth graders, excitedly compared the purchases they'd just made at a computer superstore. I was familiar with the titles, all violent action games. I was struck more by the amount of money they'd just spent—at least $120 apiece—than by the nature of the games, which are certainly popular with kids that age. Did they have software allowances? Was this the grand culmination of a year of mowing lawns, shoveling snow, and the like? Judging from their casual attitudes, it seemed that such buying expeditions weren't uncommon.

I suspect that their parents simply accepted the cost of the software as a reality of the digital age. Twenty-nine dollars is about the smallest sum with which you can ante up to the software table. So maybe allowing your kids to drop a hundred bucks is all right, as long as it's for the noble cause of feeding the computer.

The key point for parents is the ease with which the computer can distort our sense of money. Whatever your software budget, don't lose sight of the high cost of software relative to your family's other discretionary spending. Even if money is no object to you, you'll do your kids a service by reminding them that each acquisition needs to be carefully considered. Chapter 6 provides a process for making solid decisions about what's worth plunking down your hard-earned cash to buy.

Another money-related issue bears some discussion: so-called obsolescence. I hear lots of kids apologizing for the computers they use at home: "My folks only have a 133 MHz Pentium or Mac IIc," "We only have 16 megs of RAM," "We just have a fourteen-inch monitor—I wish they'd just buy a new one." About the only thing more embarrassing would be to admit that they live in a house with a black-and-white television or a rotary phone. Never mind that these kids have more computing power than the governments of many developing countries have!

This mentality is not surprising, given an industry that often refers to recent previous models as dinosaurs, a term that would be perfectly understandable if we were talking about room-sized models, circa 1945. But today, *obsolete* can easily describe last year's, or even last quarter's, state-of-the-art machines. It takes very little for the pundits to sound the death knell for a previous generation of chips. And it takes very little for us to believe them; we're almost conditioned to salivate through our wallets when marketers ring the new-product bell. You, and ultimately your children, will benefit if you extinguish your conditioned response to announcements of obsolescence. There's only one real measure of obsolescence: Does the machine run current software in a fashion that creates a satisfying computing experience? If so, your computer isn't obsolete, and your kids need to know that.

## Media by Any Other Name

With all the excitement over computers, it's easy to convey the message to our kids that electronic media are *better* than traditional media—painting on the screen is better than using pens, markers, crayons, and paper; reading an interactive book on the computer is better than reading a printed book, and so on.

In fact, it is more helpful to our children for digital media to complement, rather than displace, traditional media. For certain, you can manipulate color, space, and texture with a computerized paint program in ways that you could never do with paper and pigments (or could do only with great skill and effort). But even with drawing tablets, which allow you to enter data into the computer with a cordless pen rather than by mouse or keyboard, you're still one step removed from a tangible creation that you can hang on the wall. You're also removed from the tactile involvement with the media that has defined art as we've known it since the early days of cave painting. It would be a shame if our children grew up in a world in which traditional techniques of painting and drawing seemed quaint or anachronistic compared to the clean and efficient capabilities of the computer.

The same holds true for books. An interactive book based on hypertext is not a replacement for a traditional linear book. Different? Yes. Fun and exciting? Often. A higher form of communication? No. As Dr. Richard Venezky, a leading expert on reading and cognitive development, points out, "The interactive book is a carryover from the deconstructionist school of literary criticism, which holds that interpretation is culturally bound, and that everyone's opinion is just as valid as the author's. But there's a good reason that we read great authors from beginning to end: We want to learn what they have to say and how they've built their arguments. Today, there's a notion that hypertext will liberate us from the shackles of linear thinking. That's just a smoke screen for the sad fact that children aren't being taught to think linearly. For hypertext or any other form of communication to be useful, you have to be able to formulate and follow linear constructs. Then a nonlinear excursion to notes, comments, references, and the like can be integrated into a meaningful structure. I'm not concerned that the book as we know it is in danger of becoming extinct."

When parents compare traditionally crafted books, paintings, drawings, or music with computer-generated products, the operant word ought to be *different*, not better. Sometimes that's hard to convey, since adults often find computers so much more efficient. I wouldn't dream of running my business with pencil and paper; creating spreadsheets and maintaining my accounts electronically has become second nature. I can't imagine organizing my research with index cards when I've developed relational databases that allow me to access whatever I need instantaneously. Nor would I begin writing a book in longhand or with a manual typewriter. At the same time, I know how to create and maintain paper ledgers and how to reconcile bank accounts. I know how to organize information with index cards. And I know how to write books and articles with nothing but a pencil and a few pads of paper.

When we push computers on children for the sake of efficiency, we run the risk of skipping the *how* and the *why* and cutting straight to the end result. Yes, it's liberating for a child to be able to type a story if he or she struggles with handwriting. And it's liberating for a child to be able to use a spreadsheet to analyze and interpret data and to move on to thinking about whole systems. But are we really helping our kids if they don't understand the fundamentals of basic math or statistics?

The bottom line is that we need to carefully position technology in our children's lives as an enhancement; otherwise, it may well rob our kids of the opportunity to participate in a tradition of communication and learning that has served us well for so many years.

## *"Just Good Enough" Syndrome*

During some research for a column on kids, computers, and homework, I interviewed a fifteen-year-old whom I'll call Claire. Was the computer helpful to her schoolwork, I asked. "Oh yes," she gushed. "Now I just search my CD-ROM [encyclopedia], and I've got it all. I don't have to go to the library to look through books anymore."

Yikes! Will someone please take this child to the library and cure her of what Mike Lawrence, a former television reporter who covered technology issues, calls the "just good enough" syndrome. According to Lawrence, "The computer is both a blessing and a curse, because it makes it so easy to target what you're looking for. Kids are willing to take the information they find and say, 'That's it.' There's no need to look any further."

Unfortunately, it's tempting for kids to regard electronic information sources as ultimate reference works because of their multimedia elements and ease of access. Sure, poorly motivated or poorly directed students have always taken minimalist approaches to research, and you might ask if there's really a difference between relying solely on a book or solely on a piece of plastic. I think there is. Although it's hard to rationalize that you've done a good job when you use just one book out of hundreds in a library, many kids truly believe that electronic references have everything they need. After all, it's the modern, post-print way of finding information. Or as Claire explained, all the cross-references on the disk make it "unnecessary" to look for information anywhere else. She forgot that the cross-references all point to items from the same source. Someone needs to encourage her to compare the information on disk with other print and electronic reference works and then apply critical thinking to fit the pieces together and synthesize multiple points of view.

Claire and her peers may well be able to have it all from a single information source in the not-too-distant future. But when they do, it will still take a lot of parentware and teacherware to ensure that students learn to translate all that data into real knowledge and insight.

## *The Myth of the Medium*

Technology is supposed to transform us into a global society of great communicators. Far from ushering in a new epistolary age, though, computer-facilitated communication seems to be contributing to a general decline in the quality of thought and language. First, the medium encourages people to instantly react—it's just so easy to whip off an email message without really thinking about what you're going to say or how you're going to frame it.

And it's even easier to fire off a response to a message; just type in what you're feeling and invoke the *reply* option. You don't even have to think about addressing the response. It's no wonder that e-mails tend to be so emotional, and that senders often regret firing off a knee-jerk response.

Second, the medium seems to engender the notion that formal language is passé. I'm astounded by the abysmal quality of correspondence I receive from professionals who know proper writing conventions. When I occasionally print out and show my colleagues their e-mail messages, some simply shrug and say, "Oh, that's just e-mail. I'd never do that in *writing*." Has the electronic medium really become the message?

It's not just adults who feel that way. As one teenager explained to me, "When you're on the Net or doing e-mail, words slow things down—they're just a wrapper. I want to get right to the information, to the meat. Who cares about the wrapper?"

That's scary stuff. Because without a good wrapper, the communication will certainly get spoiled.

## *Summary*

Beware of the tendency of the computer to distort children's (and adults') sense of time, speed, power, and money. Talk with your kids about these issues and your concerns. Reinforce the idea that the real machine is the one between their ears, and that the here and now of the real world can be a pretty exciting place.

Chapter 5

# The Smart PC Shopper

## Buying the Right Stuff

### *Taking the Plunge*

I'll do just about anything to avoid going into computer superstores, although on a Saturday evening at eight, when
I'm fresh out of toner cartridges for the laser printer and on
deadline, they're lifesavers. During one evening visit, forced
by a leaky cartridge, I did a little market research for this
book by sauntering over to the computer systems area to observe people shopping for their first home computer.

On the way, through an open door, I saw a group of first-
time buyers at an introductory course that the store offers
prospective and new customers. The students (mostly forty-
and fiftysomethings) looked about as comfortable as if they
were getting a one-hour crash course in cardiac surgery before going in to perform a quadruple bypass.

In the systems aisle, a couple approached a salesman and
asked for help. They said they wanted something that would

run reference software, home finance software, and games. The salesperson immediately launched a salvo of technical information, some correct, some off the mark, and then recommended a machine. The couple looked at the computer for a few minutes, then asked which credit cards the store accepted. About ten minutes later they were in the checkout line, the boxes from their new acquisition piled in a shopping cart like so many groceries.

I hope they bought the right machine, given that they bought it the wrong way, namely, by going into a store cold and depending on a salesperson's advice. To be sure, there are qualified computer salesfolk out there who will give you good buying advice—but you can't always count on it. I've been given outrageously wrong information by well-meaning, but technically ignorant salespeople (one told me that the fatter your printer cable, the faster your printer will print. Right. And a pound of chicken fat falls faster than a pound of chicken feathers!). So the onus is on *you* to make good hardware purchases for your family. If you buy at the very low end, you might not be able to run the latest software; the minimum requirements level keeps rising as software gets more complex.

In this chapter, I've provided some straightforward guidelines that will enable you to learn how to make good hardware purchasing decisions. I've avoided mentioning specific makes and models, since manufacturers are coming out with new wares every month. More important, I've tried to provide a generic blueprint for making wise purchasing decisions.

## *Get Smart First, Buy Second*

Next to your house and car, a computer is probably going to be one of the most expensive acquisitions you'll make. You wouldn't buy a house or car without careful research, and the same forethought ought to go into buying your family a PC. If you just walk into a store cold, you'll likely leave confused, or with a trunk weighted down with computer gear that may or may not fit your needs. You might underbuy; you might overbuy—neither is desirable, if you underbuy, you'll probably have an unsatisfying experience with your home PC and wind up paying a lot of extra cash to upgrade later on. If you overbuy, you'll be wasting your hard-earned greenbacks on options and/or functionality you simply do not need.

It's important to know about the basic components (processor chip, memory, hard disk, video card, etc.) you'll find under the hood of any computer, regardless of the manufacturer. It's also important to gain a sense of where technology has been and where it's going. The industry can change on a dime, and a piece of equipment that looks promising in one month may be a dead end six months later. How will you learn about all this stuff without getting a Ph.D. in electrical engineering? The fact is, you don't need to know a whole lot to buy or to use computers effectively. You don't need to know about electrons or the principles of magnetism that allow your hard disk to store data, or how the laser in your CD-ROM drive reads data off a piece of plastic. And you certainly don't need to learn programming—the software publishers have taken care of all the ones and zeroes (the basic building blocks of computer languages).

Many of the computer magazines run comparative reviews of computer systems. These can be helpful for getting a general sense of what kinds of components and specifications give you the most computer for your money. Don't worry if the performance charts don't mean anything to you; sometimes they don't mean much to the experts, at least in terms of real-world experience. If a hard disk in one computer can retrieve data one millisecond (that's one-thousandth of a second) faster than that in another machine, will anyone notice a difference? Unlikely. Read for generalities about current standards for

- hard disk size
- memory (RAM)
- computer speed
- CD-ROM drives
- modems
- monitor size
- back-up media

Also, pay close attention to the advertisements, and observe the following:

- the components included with each kind of computer
- the features the computer manufacturers are touting as important
- the similarities among computers in the same price range

You'll need this kind of information when you get down to making a purchasing decision. An introductory course on computing can be extremely valuable even before you buy, so you can get a feel for what your new computer can do. The course should be geared toward general micro-computing. Check out listings for your town's adult education programs, as well as classes sponsored by private training companies. However you learn about computers, you'll be much better equipped to make a sensible purchase for your family. And you won't feel like you're at the mercy of others who hold the knowledge key to a mysterious black box.

## *Know What You Want*

Any computer you buy today will have the basics you need to run multimedia software: the computer itself, monitor, CD-ROM drive, and sound card. Many also include (cheap) speakers as well, so you'll be ready to set up and run your machine as soon as you get it home. Still, there are choices you'll have to make, especially if you purchase by mail order and have a computer made to your specifications. You also will have to select from many preconfigured systems that increase in price as they increase in power and storage capacity.

Make sure that the CD-ROM drive is the current standard (again, compare ads in the magazines, since the state of the art changes so quickly) and that the speakers offer quality sound reproduction; listen before you buy. You'll also probably want a modem so you can access the Internet or online services. Get one with the fastest capabilities available at the time of purchase (you'll recognize the slower ones because they'll be considerably less expensive). If you're buying the computer for your kids, a color printer is a *must* to take advantage of paint, draw, and other creativity programs. Kids are used to creating projects and expressing themselves with vivid colors. The good news is that the prices on color printers are constantly dropping, and even an inexpensive color printer's output can be stunning.

Once you have your basic setup, you get into the realm of the definitely optional but definitely fun. Scanners designed to handle small color photos, and digital cameras are both in this category. They enable you to use the computer in new and exciting ways, and both have definite utilitarian functions as well.

## *Desktop or Laptop*

In general, if you're only going to have one computer, it's better to buy a desktop than a laptop. You need to spend a significant amount of money on a laptop in order to duplicate the amenities and expandability of a desktop system. Even a low-end laptop will cost at least as much as, and probably slightly more, than a desktop computer with greater capacity and power. And while the screens of many laptops are excellent, no laptop display will match that of a good monitor.

Still, if you can find a deal on a laptop with a good screen, you might want to consider it for your child. (You'll have a choice of passive or active matrix; go with the active matrix—the colors are much brighter.) The laptop should have a CD-ROM drive and enough memory to run current software.

Some people find that there are advantages to going the laptop route when the computer will be used by a child. The smaller keyboard is a plus for small hands, and since the computer is portable, your child can do homework in the kitchen or living room or wherever the rest of the family members are hanging out.

Caveat: If you do buy a laptop, read the battery-charging instructions carefully and train your child accordingly. Some types of batteries will get overcharged if you run the computer continuously from the AC adapter. You need to know when to unplug and run off the batteries, and when to recharge. It's hard for kids to remember all the charging rules, and you can greatly shorten the life of the computer's expensive battery.

## Don't Forget the Furniture

Typically, computer furniture is an afterthought or takes second place to the actual machine. It's worth thinking about up front, for logistical and health reasons. It's relatively simple to have a good ergonomic workplace in your home. It just takes a bit of advance planning. A computer resting on a table will likely be poor placement for everyone. When you're at the keyboard, your arms should be bent at the elbow at a ninety-degree angle. Your hands should be placed on the keyboard so that your fingers naturally drop down on the keys. At the same time, your eyes should be slightly above the middle of the screen.

To achieve this combination, you'll either need a computer desk with a keyboard drawer, or you'll need to add a keyboard drawer to an existing table or desk. You'll also want an adjustable-height chair so that your kid's feet are flat on the floor. If you can't find a short enough chair, put a footrest or stack of phone books under your child's feet. With an adjustable chair, everyone can have the proper sitting position.

The good news is that computer furniture is relatively inexpensive and unobtrusive. You can usually find good deals on computer desks and chairs at a superstore or a discount office supply store. Hunt around and you might even find something that fits in with your décor (if your playroom motif is like ours, early Halloween, then anything can go!).

Why bother with the ergonometric furniture? For adults, repetitive strain injuries are well documented. Even if you don't have an injury, you'll enjoy your time at the computer more if your wrists aren't sore and your neck doesn't hurt. There's no documentation that kids are subject to the same problems as grownups. But then again, we've never raised a PC generation. Why not establish good sitting and viewing habits now with your kids, and provide the wherewithal to do so? It will only help your kids when they enter the workforce, and it will certainly be more comfortable for them as their bodies become less supple.

An added advantage of a computer table with a keyboard drawer is that it forces your kids to stay farther away from the monitor. There's still a lot of controversy about the potentially harmful effects of low-level electromagnetic emissions from monitors, and almost all name-brand monitors meet basic low-level compliance standards (called MPR II). An increasing number of monitors also meet a Swedish standard called TCO95, which allows for roughly half of the MPR II levels. (The Swedes are much more concerned about low-level emissions and have much more stringent guidelines.)

My position is that there's no point waiting for a definitive scientific conclusion about the issue. Keeping your child's head (and your own) a couple of feet from the monitor is a reasonable safety measure. In our house, I've attached an extended-keyboard drawer to a computer table and pushed the monitor to the back edge of the tabletop, ensuring that my children and their friends stay about two feet from the screen. The kids actually like it that way, because no one can hog the show by shoving his or her head smack in front of the monitor.

## *Stay off the Bleeding Edge of Technology*

Do you aspire to be the first on your block to own a robotic lawnmower or neutron-powered garden weeder? In marketing lingo, are you an early adopter? If so, you might want to drop back to second place next time you hear about a new whiz-bang computer product, or when a salesperson tries to sell you one.

When you buy the latest technology, you pay premium prices. Competition eventually drives the price down, so if you can control your urge to own the newest state-of-the-art gear, you can hang onto your money until the innovation becomes more commonplace. There are several good reasons to keep your wallet in your pocket for a while, at least until prices drop and kinks are worked out of the product.

First, the latest and greatest can be the most finicky to

work with. As I've learned the hard way, revolutionary technology is often a major time sink and a source of migraine headaches. Then there's the compatibility issue. A manufacturer might offer a product that no one else supports yet, or for which standards haven't been proposed. The rule of thumb is this: When it comes to new technology, let others be the guinea pigs.

## Buy at the Right Time

Believe it or not, there's a right time and a wrong time to buy a new computer. Timing your entry into the computer world means trying to get the most benefit out of the latest technology without having to pay through the nose for it. Historically, new digital technology (a chip or system design) starts off very expensive, then gets cheaper as factories ramp up production and companies sell more units. Another new technology then supplants its predecessor, and the cycle repeats itself. It's important here to distinguish between two types of advances.

The first is major microchip or system design that enables the computer to process more data at faster speeds. For example, on the PC side, the introduction of the Pentium II chip (the fastest chip available at the time of this writing) represents a quantum leap in computing power over the previous generation (the 486 chip). On the Macintosh side, the PowerPC chip represents an equally large jump over previous generation of chips.

The second type of change, call it incremental, takes

place within a particular chip family—say, a jump from a Pentium II 233 to a Pentium II 266 (the number, stated in megahertz, or MHz, is a measure of how fast the chip processes data). This type of change offers much smaller definite improvements in computing power. Ask the sales rep for information about the percentage improvement, and compare the answers against information in the computer magazines.

So what's the timing on all this? Traditionally, major changes in chip design take place every twelve to eighteen months; incremental improvements can occur every few months. What this means for you, the consumer, is that prices on computers tend to drop about six months after the introduction of a new chip, and a month or two after an incrementally improved chip. This isn't to say you should wait for a new chip plus six months; prices are tumbling all the time and you can buy a remarkable amount of horsepower for less than $1,000. But if a new chip has been released within the last four months and you can wait to buy a new PC, you'll probably enjoy significant savings by hanging on a bit.

## Buy for the Long Haul

How long should you expect your home computer purchase to last? A reasonable time is three years. That doesn't mean you have to toss your machine into the trash heap when you've hit the two years eleven months mark. And it doesn't mean that you may not make significant upgrades to your machine before the three years are up. Still, three years is the most cost-effective time frame for planning your computer purchases.

If you buy for three years, and you pay about $2,100 (which will purchase a *lot* of computer these days), then you're spending about $700 a year, maybe a little more when you add some extra components and replacement parts. That doesn't count the software you'll want to purchase over time; a safe estimate for budgeting purposes would be one program a month at about $40 each. That adds up to about $1,200 a year. At the end of three years, you may be ready for another machine, but your old one will still be good enough for your kids to share, especially if you can make a sensible upgrade (larger hard disk, more memory, faster CD-ROM drive, and perhaps an accelerated video card). In this way, you're likely to amortize your expense beyond the three-year mark.

## Buy at the Right Place

Once you decide what kind of PC to buy, and you know how much to spend and what to look for, you need to decide where to buy the machine. As a consumer, you have a number of options, and the one you select really depends on the level of help you think you may need before and after you buy. Effective customer support that can help resolve operational questions and problems (what cables go where, what to do when your computer freezes or *hangs,* etc.), and a repair shop make owning a PC more comfortable. Informed and helpful salespeople are another vital link in your purchase decision. If you don't know very much about computers, then you'll need expert and sympathic sales help. Finally, there's price. If you know your way around the world of computers, the bottom line might be all that matters to you. Here's how the various sales venues compare on prices, service, and support.

Warehouse electronic stores (like warehouse food stores) often have great prices, but little, if any, sales help. Also, their selection is typically limited to a few brands. Various options for systems configurations may be unavailable; that is, they may not be able to unbundle items you don't want, like cheap speakers, slow modems, or slow CD-ROM drives. Don't expect service or support after you take your PC home, except whatever's provided in the manufacturer's warranty. (These days, a good warranty covers the gear for two or three years. Manufacturers can afford such long-term coverage because digital electronic equipment tends to either arrive brain dead or last for many years.)

Computer superstores (supermarket-size stores that sell computer gear) will provide training, support, and repair services, but they won't be as cheap as warehouse stores or mail-order outlets. The quality of advice can range from excellent to horrendous. So it's important to know what you want before shopping in a superstore, or at least know what to ask. Again, read the magazines or talk with knowledgeable friends. Armed with good information, you'll usually be able to work with the sales staff of a superstore to find what you need, and rest assured knowing that whatever you buy can be fixed or upgraded on the premises.

Office supply discounters usually carry computers, but generally don't provide a high level of support. Typically they send your computer to the manufacturer (or have you do so) if there's a problem. Nonetheless, if support isn't an issue, you can often find good deals at these vendors.

Mail-order computer manufacturers definitely offer the most options. Each makes its own line of computers, usually to your own specifications. You choose the processor, the size of the drive, the amount of memory, and so on, and they ship it to you. The salespeople tend to be highly knowledgeable and helpful: State what you want to do with the computer, and they can generally put together a system that you won't outgrow for a while. Also, the technical support, via telephone, is usually good to top-notch. Some of the mail-order companies offer excellent on-site service contracts for relatively small amounts of money. If you're not comfortable opening the box and tinkering with your computer's innards, this might be a worthwhile expenditure.

Software/hardware mail-order companies sometimes sell a house brand, but typically also carry well-known makes and models, particularly laptops. Prices are often low; but technical support is designed largely to help you resolve problems, not to provide basic help with a system. For the experienced user, this option is generally a good one; novice computer users, however, might feel left in the dark.

To sum up: Choose a type of vendor on the basis of how much support you'll need during the purchase and after the buy. The more you know beforehand, the greater your options will be for picking and choosing purchasing outlets when you're ready to pull out your credit card.

# Don't Look for Free Bytes

When you're looking at computer advertisements or prowling the aisles of your local computer superstore, it's almost impossible not to be seduced by the added equipment and software that some computer makers throw into the mix to make their systems seem like a better deal. Some of the tossed-in goodies are worthwhile; others aren't worth the plastic they're made of.

For example, unless you're buying an expensive system, the speakers tossed into the deal are generally terrible, producing tinny and shallow sound reminiscent of old transistor radios. Listen to the speakers running with the type of software you'll be using before you buy. If you don't like what you hear, ask if you can upgrade or if you can buy the system without them.

In short, it's up to you to make sure you're purchasing a computer that is up to snuff in terms of specifications. And the only way you can guarantee that is by educating yourself about what specs constitute the state of the art and what brands are considered industry standards. Then act accordingly.

# Beware of Computer Salespeople Bearing Chips

There are some common-sense rules to buying computers that apply to just about all purchases. If you see a deal in a new computer system that's too good to be true, it is, and you should stay as far away from it as possible.

So do your homework and then buy brands you trust from reputable dealers. The preliminary research can take some time, especially if you're a first-time buyer. And you'll never know for sure that you bought the right system for a reasonable price at the best possible time. But, by putting in the effort now and using the common-sense principles you'd apply to any major purchase, you should walk away a satisfied customer—and the owner of a computer that will serve you and your family for several years to come.

## *Make Smart Upgrades*

So far I've discussed purchasing new systems. But what if you want to give your PC a shot in the arm before its three-year cycle is complete? Your computer's memory or hard disk space may be insufficient for a new generation of software. You might need a faster video card to better handle animation and sound. Once it's clear that you need to upgrade your system, you also need to calculate whether it's worth the cost. There's also the aggravation factor: If you don't have the technical knowledge required to work "under the hood" installing new components or swapping old ones, you might need a friend or a hired expert to help out.

As a general rule, the following kinds of upgrades make sense: adding memory, storage, and video to ease up performance bottlenecks, faster CD-ROM or higher-quality audio gear to enhance your enjoyment, and a scanner or digital camera to allow you to use the computer in a new way.

To avoid being disappointed from the results of your upgrade, it's important to make sensible choices. If you're about to completely rehab an older computer by replacing the microprocessor chip, hard disk, memory, and video card, you'd be better off spending the cash for a new machine. With the plummeting costs and rising power of PCs, you'll probably enjoy far better performance than "old faithful" would deliver with its new innards.

Also, be aware that upgrades have a way of insidiously escalating, even if you start out with a firm resolution to hold the line at a certain amount. You start off with a $250 expenditure for a larger or second hard disk, then decide that you might as well add more RAM, too. So you up the bottom line by another $100 or so. At that point, you see some performance improvement and want to go for a processor upgrade, which might cost you another $200 or more. Later, you realize that the video is dragging you down, so you opt for a new graphics adapter. Before long, you've rehabbed the entire machine!

## Buy Used with Caution

With prices falling as quickly as they do, and with upgrading a possibility, it generally doesn't make a lot of sense to buy a used computer. Still, if you need a second computer for a student at home, or for letter writing and household budgeting, you can often get by with a used machine. An older, but functioning, computer might be perfect for a student to write papers or to do research, especially if you outfit it with a CD-ROM drive and a modem.

The key considerations with a used PC are its condition and the guarantee. Here is a checklist of questions to ask and things to look for when buying used:

1. When was the computer purchased?
2. Is the machine still under warranty? (The seller might have to contact the manufacturer to indicate new ownership.) And what kind of warranty will the seller offer?
3. Where was the computer used (office, home, home office)?
4. What repairs and/or upgrades were made, and does the seller have receipts or paperwork?
5. Does the seller have all the manuals, cables, and accessories that came with the original machine?

The safest place to buy a used PC is a computer store that refurbishes secondhand machines and offers at least a ninety-day guarantee. If you buy a computer from an individual through a classified ad, ask for any repair records. You might also want to have a consultant or more knowledgeable friend give an opinion as to the computer's condition. If you can get some kind of guarantee, all the better. And with a complicated instrument like a computer, never sign a bill of sale that says you're taking the computer "as is."

Wherever you buy a used computer, remember that the little things—manuals, mouse, keyboard cord, power cords, cables, and the like—make a difference. The more complete the system, the less hassle for you in getting up and running.

# *Summary*

If the world of hardware seems confusing to you, you're not alone; new equipment seems to hit the shelves almost daily. Nonetheless, you can make wise purchases if you arm yourself with current information about standards and going prices. Read the current computer magazines, talk to knowledgeable friends, and compare the recommendations of various salespeople. The more you know, the better your chances of buying a computer that will serve your family well for the next several years.

*Chapter 6*

# Bits and Bytes

## Buying Software for Your Kids

### *A Matter of Taste*

Ordinarily, I don't pay too much attention to computer games, especially the "slice 'em and dice 'em" variety. All that changed when the producers of the television show *48 Hours* asked me to round up some of the best and worst programs to present to its viewing audience during a taped segment. I had plenty of quality programs to demo, but needed to get hold of a few programs representing the opposite end of the spectrum. So I headed for the nearest retail software store and asked the person at the cash register, Jerry, to show me the best action CDs.

Before Jerry could answer, another salesperson, Ron, who had overheard our conversation, bounded back from the stockroom with a stack of boxes in hand. "This," he panted as he waved one in front of me, "is *exactly* what you want."

"Why's that?" I asked as I studied the box, which featured

a fierce-looking woman and three fierce commando types all firing fierce-looking weapons at fierce-looking enemies. The copy on the back promised more mayhem than anyone thought possible.

" 'Cause if you aim the bazooka at an enemy's head, his eyeballs splatter on the screen," Ron answered, his own eyes bulging.

"Wow! Just my kinda game," I deadpanned. I then paid for the eyeblasterware and several other human-garbage-disposal games and thanked my enthusiastic buddy for his sound advice.

Ron smiled and waved, clearly pleased that he'd earned his keep for the day. Jerry acknowledged his colleague's good taste in software with a nod, and walked over to help another customer.

So much for soliciting a software salesperson's opinion about which programs to buy. Of course, everyone's entitled to his or her own ideas about what makes for a good software package. And like anything else, a software program's beauty lies in the eyes of the mouse holder. Which is why you really need to make your own decisions about what's worthwhile and appropriate for your children. In other words, you need to become your family's in-house software purchasing agent and reviewer. This chapter teaches you how to do just that by explaining what kinds of programs are available, and what kinds of hard questions you ought to ask before making a software purchase.

Before you launch into the review process, I recommend adopting a "show-me" mindset. This is important, because the old saw "You can't judge a book by its cover" applies in gigabytes to the world of software. As many people learn after getting burned a few times, the gap between the claims on the box and the reality of the plastic inside can be astounding—as is the number of programs that never should have been pressed onto plastic! (These titles are often referred to as *shovelware,* because they simply represent mounds of data mindlessly heaped onto a disk.)

A lot of children's software is created to fill a marketing niche, rather than to help kids learn. Many programs tend to be either too textbook-like or too cartoon-like. As a result, much software in the edutainment category is either not very entertaining (or entertaining for only a short time) or just paying lip service to the *edu* part.

A handful of companies have actually figured out how to make compelling and educationally sound products that are well worth the money. Even so, you can't assume that just because you like titles from a particular publisher, you'll like the company's latest release as well. Even the top makers of educational and family software occasionally unleash a dog in search of a pound.

The safest posture is to adopt a healthy skepticism about all new software, regardless of who makes it. As a software reviewer, I take what may at first seem a harsh approach: I look at the task of reviewing as a series of hurdles that the title must pass to get a high mark. If you take a similar attitude, you'll be pleasantly surprised when the software lives up to or exceeds your expectations and your children's needs.

## *A Note on Buying*

Before launching into criteria for selecting software, I want to stress a key buying strategy. In fact, if you don't read anything else in this chapter but take to heart this bit of purchasing advice, I'll feel satisfied that I've done you a good service: Don't leave the store without an MBG (money-back guarantee).

If software programming were fifty-cent-apiece throwaway items, there would be less need to be concerned with up-front researching and evaluation. You could take a buckshot approach, buying handfuls of plastic and hoping that something good would remain when you separated the dogs from the stars. But many software packages turn out to be $29, $39, and $49 throwaway items, which can add up to a lot of cash you could spend on other family investments. That's why an MBG is critical. Fortunately, a growing number of retail-software and mail-order catalogs have caught on to consumer sensitivity toward shovelware products, and offer no-questions-asked return policies. If you can't find a store or catalog that offers a money-back guarantee, buy directly from the publisher, and ask about returns before placing the order. You may pay more than you would through retail or mail order, but that extra expenditure can be well worth it. With a money-back guarantee, you'll have the peace of mind (and probably more cash) to purchase software that will be of the most value to your family members.

## *Building a Well-Rounded Software Library*

What is a software library anyway; don't you just buy what your kids need for school or packages that strike your fancy based on ads in the computing magazines?

Here's a different approach that Sally Narodick (a former educator and chief executive of Edmark Corporation, a maker of top-quality educational programs for children) recommends. She considers the acquisition of software essential to the building of computer literacy. And she defines computer literacy simply as "the state people reach when they can use the computer as a tool." Narodick believes computer literacy is desirable because computers can help both children and adults to "operate at a higher level of human potential."

To facilitate computer literacy in your household, Narodick emphasizes the importance of buying software with a plan in mind. "If you're going to treat the computer as a valuable tool, you can't just buy software helter-skelter," she warns. "You want to spend your money wisely and methodically." To this end, she recommends purchasing the following types of titles:

- Software that helps children practice basic skills in math, reading, and other subjects.
- Programs designed to facilitate writing and publishing, and to stimulate creativity.
- Software that challenges higher-order thinking skills (i.e., helps with deductive reasoning, problem solving, what-if simulations, etc.).
- Games and simulations that encourage strategy develop-

ment and an understanding of complex interrelationships within systems.

- Reference software and tools for exploring the online world.

Within each category you'll find numerous options. What are the best programs for your children? That's where the research and review process comes in. You might feel comfortable basing your choices on third-party assessments. You might prefer to start from scratch and review a potential acquisition yourself. (It's still a good idea to do some research rather than simply buying on the basis of a publisher's ad or box copy.) You'll find ideas and proven tactics below for following either course of action.

## Researching Software

The task of figuring out what's available and what's good can seem daunting and time-consuming. Here are some ways you can make the process easier and quicker, and above all, more fun for you and your kids.

- Read reviews. Get a general sense of a program you're thinking about purchasing. Read several computing magazines and compare the reviewers' comments. You'll soon get an idea of the biases and attitudes, and who tells it straight vs. who sells editorial (an industry term for magazines that say only nice things about products from publishers who advertise heavily).
- Talk to other parents. Kids often want programs because

they've used them at a friend's home. Ask the parents for their opinions. Set up a time to try the programs yourself when you drop off or pick up your child at their friends' homes.

- Talk to teachers and technology coordinators. If a teacher is actively involved with computing, he or she can probably suggest titles that have strong educational value and that will engage your child. School technology coordinators will also likely have good recommendations.
- Check out other sources. Post inquiries on bulletin boards and forums for parents and ask other parents at PTA/PTO meetings about their software choices.
- Coordinate a meeting at your child's school. Ask the principal or headmaster about setting up a technology night for people to talk about and demonstrate their favorite programs. Local computer stores or sales reps will sometimes help with the effort and can make your tech night a smashing success.
- Visit trade shows in your area. See what the latest offerings are. Most of the vendors demo their software at such events, and many will offer trial copies or discounts on full versions.
- Join local user groups in your area. You'll find them in the phone book under clubs or entertainment, if they're big enough.
- If you're already up and running, use the online services. Check out vendors' forums. Browse messages about products in which you're interested; the online community is quite vocal about its likes and dislikes. Also, look for opportunities online to download sample versions of software; there's nothing like trying before buying. Check

out publishers' Web pages; you can often download demo versions of popular kids' programs.

## Becoming an Instant Reviewer

Are you ready to join the ranks of those who put software through its paces and test the hype on the back of the box? Presumably, you've already done some research and have targeted some software packages for your review. Now you'll need to get hold of the software or view a good demo. Some stores will let you load a program on a floor model machine, or may already have popular titles on PCs throughout the store (although the popular titles tend to be action and arcade games). If you've read about a program that, based on your research, is a good candidate for your software library, buy it. Just make sure you can take it back.

As your family's in-house software reviewer, you'll need some general and specific guidelines for assessing new programs. I apply the following general criteria to all software that comes in the door for review.

1. *Good software is fun and stimulating.* It has to be engaging. Kids like to be stimulated and challenged. Any title that doesn't do both usually goes on the shelf and stays there.
2. *Good software is developmentally appropriate.* A five-year-old's capabilities are vastly different from a nine-year-old's. So when I see a software package that claims the software is appropriate for kids ranging from three to nine, my warning light begins to flash. You don't need

an advanced degree in psychology to know that broad age ranges spanning large developmental categories can't be meaningful. Beware the "one size fits (nearly) all kids" mentality.

3. *Good software is rewarding for your child.* If the reward system is based solely on beating the clock or racking up the most points, the program may not be a good fit for your child. Your child might do better with a program that allows him or her to arrive at the answer in his or her own way and time, or one that provides rewards in the form of an opportunity to create something unusual. You know what types of situations are likely to prove frustrating and which will lead to positive experiences. The trick is to apply that knowledge to the medium of software.

4. *Good software is simple and intuitive.* Life's too short to figure out convoluted software. Simplicity doesn't have to mean shallowness, however. Some of the most powerful productivity software packages are simple and easy to use. No wonder—it's a lot harder to develop an elegantly simple program than it is to thoughtlessly stuff the software with features, many of them of dubious value.

With these thoughts in mind, you can ask the following specific questions. Your answers will ultimately determine whether the software is a good choice for you and your family.

## 1. What does the software bring to the party?

People are often surprised after they ask what to look for when considering a new software package. Solid learning materials? Ease of use? Inviting graphics? Good use of multimedia? Yes, but there are other, more subtle, considerations, too.

When I review a program, the first question I answer is this: Does the software or CD-ROM simply mimic what you can do with conventional media (books and other printed material, art supplies, etc.), or does it allow children to learn, play, and manipulate reality in ways that only a computer can? Does the software really harness the unique power of the computer to present information in novel ways, to create imagery that would be impossible to create with conventional media, or to combine media in ways not possible by hand?

For example, many programs for young children contain a collection of electronic activities such as flash cards, color mixing, simple math exercises, or contain cartoon-like characters who sing and chat in squeaky voices as they guide your child around the screen. Most of these programs offer little over their traditional print counterparts, and if anything, are a waste of electricity. Your child is better off using real blocks and shape sorters, mixing colors by hand, or holding flash cards than sitting in front of a screen doing an ersatz version of the same.

On the other hand, a full-featured paint/draw program designed for children enables your kids to create colors, textures, patterns, and the like that simply couldn't exist off the screen. Better still, these programs let young artists create their own visions of reality. Who says you can't find forests of purple lollipops surrounded by singing gingerbread cookies and neatly trimmed beds of orange Ping-Pong balls? If your kids can imagine it, they can bring their vision to life onscreen, print it out, and perhaps incorporate it into a family letterhead, a personal-journal entry, or even a desktop-published novel.

Bottom line? If the software amounts to an electronic version of traditional media, skip it and save your money for boxes of crayons, books, trips to museums, and video rentals. When it comes to buying software, hold out for the high-value programs that make your expenditure, and your kids' efforts, worth it.

## 2. Does anyone really need this thing?

This question asks whether this subject is worth our kids' time. Does it enhance their knowledge base? Does it challenge their problem-solving skills?

As you'll discover, the subject matter of CDs ranges from broad treatment of a subject—say, the oceans, space, or a painting genre—to a laser-like focus on a single topic. Believe it or not, I once reviewed an entire CD-ROM dedicated to teaching children to use less salt! (How about sharing five minutes to discuss the issue with your children and then setting a good example in the kitchen?)

You can find various CDs that take your children on journeys through time and space, or that teach history, important principles of physics, concepts in art history, and the like. In short, the worthiness of the CD is a blend of the content and its presentation, and it all comes down to the question: Would you buy a product in any medium concerned with this topic?

## 3. Does it offer meaningful interactivity?

If I had a dime for every parent who's said, "I really like the fact that my kids spend time at the computer rather than in front of the television, because computers are interactive," I'd have a lot of money. But if I had a dollar for every software package that was interactive in a meaningful sense, I'd be pretty hungry.

No word is more bandied about in computing than *interactive*—interactive games, interactive reference works, interactive movies, interactive books. Interactivity is the promise of computing and is upheld as one of the key differentiators between PCs and TVs. With television, you and your kids sit in front of the screen like sponges, passively soaking in the rays. With computers, you're supposed to be able to get in on the act. Interact, that is.

Unfortunately, interactivity is a slippery concept, and the term has become a great marketing buzzword. At the most basic level, interactivity implies a degree of control that users can exercise over the software. The question, though, is whether the control is meaningful. After all, by definition, the computer is interactive; you have to use the keyboard, mouse, or other input device to make the machine do anything at all. But at what point does that input shape a better learning or entertainment experience? And when does it become counterproductive (as when a child sits glassy-eyed while clicking on the same object five hundred times)? To answer these questions, consider two extremes.

At one end, we have the typical electronic book, which is interactive because your children can choose to listen to a narrated version of a story, or they can elect to bop around the text by themselves, clicking on various items on the screen to make amusing things happen, like a cow jumping out of a hole in a tree. The amusement is typically short-lived, though, and kids tire of such games easily. Is this really an improvement over noninteractive cartoons or television? I don't think so. In fact, it doesn't necessarily place the computer all that far above television, if at all. Yes, your child gets to click a button to start the show or to take minor detours as the software proceeds along its course, but he or she doesn't really gain any knowledge, skill, or insight in the process. Such interactivity is hardly a worthy rationale for buying the software.

At the other extreme, consider programs such as SimCity, which are almost entirely user driven; everything the user does affects the outcome of the game. Players make numerous decisions (such as managing resources in a metropolis or rainforest), determining the flow of the game, and shaping the computing experience as they proceed. The interactivity helps sharpen decision-making skills by giving kids a no-risk arena in which they can test scenarios and note the consequences.

In between, you'll find a gaggle of software with claims of interactivity plastered all over the boxes. Don't take it for granted that the programs offer useful interaction. Try them yourself and see whether the interactivity really adds value, allowing your kids to actively participate with and direct the program. Good software encourages children to observe and listen, process information, and develop and test their ideas on screen.

I have no doubt that in years to come, interactivity will be better developed in all software genres, including those related to children. In fact, meaningful interactivity will inevitably become a competitive tool; publishers that offer programs with solid interactive components will be among the most successful. In the meantime, understand the limitations of interactivity and base your software acquisitions on what the programs can actually do for your family. When you take a disk for a test spin, let the "wow, this is cool" feeling pass, and see if the interactivity amounts to anything more than a minor involvement with the flow of the program. If it boils down to TV, then place it back on the shelf and let it be; the last thing we need is a generation of junior keyboard potatoes.

## 4. Will it keep?

As the best expert on your children, you're in a good position to predict whether the software will be a perennial hit, or a flash in the drive. Some kids won't mind covering the same ground again and again, and may enjoy listening to a CD tell a story or clicking on a toaster for the ninety-seventh time to eject a bicycling whale. But based on anecdotal information from parents, the tendency is for kids to get bored quickly. It's not uncommon to hear complaints from parents about the "cost per hour" of the software. Remember, you're not talking about free TV or three-dollar comic books; a steady need for new CD-ROMs to maintain your child's interest can quickly become a very expensive habit.

What makes for good shelf life? Programs with the longest shelf life tend to be open-ended, or to have enough permutations so that your children won't exhaust the possibilities early on. Graphics programs by definition will be open-ended, and will have a long shelf life if they provide rich and unusual tools. Mystery games can interest kids for months if the case can't be cracked with a universal approach or small inventory of sleuthing techniques. Strategy games such as Oregon Trail offer many hours of challenging fun. In short, look for programs that have lots of possibilities to keep your kids from shrugging "been there, done that" too quickly.

Another factor in software's shelf life is the variability of its challenge level. The more control and opportunity for upping the challenge your kids have, the more likely the software will continue to interest and grow with them as their abilities and interests change. (Some software packages give you more bytes for the buck, because younger or older siblings can tailor the games to their capabilities.)

Certain programs, by their nature, have a limited lifespan. For example, you might want to replace an annually updated encyclopedia, dictionary, or atlas. But these programs are exceptions to the rule that good software shouldn't come with expiration dates. As a general principle, you should buy only those programs that you believe will stick around your family's active library long enough to earn their keep.

## 5. Does it provide good opportunities to coach and mentor?

As you acquire software, look for what Edmark's Sally Narodick and general manager Donna Stanger call "teachable moments"—instances when you can ask good questions. "The art of great teaching is asking thoughtful and well-timed questions," Narodick says, putting on her educator's cap. "If the software provides challenging activities, you can stop and ask questions like, 'Wow, that's great, how did you ever figure that out?' That opens the door for your children to think about and verbalize the process they used to solve a problem or devise a strategy. And by helping children to think about the 'hows' and not just the 'whats,' you really help them reflect on the thinking process and cement their learning so they can generalize skills to other situations."

## 6. Does the program teach or just bleep?

When a software title requires closed-ended answers (e.g., the correct answer to a math problem), will it offer kids enough feedback, such as suggestions for formulating another try, or will it simply tell them they're wrong? A program that only beeps or buzzes doesn't lend a lot to the learning process. Also, how frequently, and meaningfully, does the program positively reinforce your children's efforts? Feedback and reinforcement are essential elements of a good learning experience, whether in the class or in front of the monitor.

Worthwhile software should reward your child for actions that merit reward. Remember, kids aren't easily fooled; if a program makes great fanfare out of something minor, your child will catch on and become suspicious. So as you examine a new disk, ask yourself, if you were a child, would you feel patronized or praised for your hard work and efforts? Then, vote on the package with your wallet.

## *Software Ratings*

So far in this section I've avoided any discussions of violent software games, which I lump in the same category as violent movies or television. It seems paradoxical that we bemoan the state of the world after reading the headlines in the morning newspaper, and then allow our kids to entertain themselves by watching mayhem onscreen. Virtual violence may not stimulate your children to create real violence, but playing games that reward them for mutilating an opponent can't possibly add anything positive to their process of learning conflict resolution. This also applies to games based solely on shooting things out of the sky.

At the same time, it's hard to keep tabs on every program that your child wants to play or buy, and violence-based freeware and shareware abound. You can certainly assess whether a software program is appropriate for your household once it's up on the screen; but unless the box depicts guts flying across the screen or scantily clad Amazonian warriors, it's sometimes hard to tell exactly what's on the disk.

Moreover, what constitutes an acceptable game in one household might be unthinkable in another. Which brings us to the concept of software ratings. These days, you'll see an increasing number of software products that sport ratings for levels of violence, nudity and/or sex, and offensive language. But as a parent, can you trust the ratings? After all, you've probably seen PG films that you thought should have been given a more stringent assessment. One intriguing rating system was created by Dr. Arthur Pober, executive director of the Entertainment Software Ratings Board (ESRB), a trade organization that the industry uses to police itself. "A good rating system provides parents with the most accurate possible information, so that they can make informed decisions," he says. "Ultimately, a good rating system means no surprises."

To create a no-surprises system, Pober studied rating approaches used in countries around the world, then devised a unique blind-testing system, somewhat akin to jury duty. ESRB trained more than a hundred testers, representing a diverse group of people ranging from students to retired school principals. When a software publisher submits a title (either the complete product or videotapes of sample portions), ESRB's computer randomly selects three names. The testers, who are paid $100 each for a session, apply their extensive criteria to the title. If at least two testers concur, the review is sent back to the publisher with the suggested evaluation; otherwise, ESRB runs another test. The publisher can accept the findings, change the offending content, or appeal the rating altogether. At the time of this writing, no publisher has chosen the appeals route. That's a good sign of the fairness of the ESRB, given the fact that it has rated more than 800 software games and 900 video titles.

The ESRB evaluations, which you'll see on many software boxes, are unique in that they offer two types of information: ratings categories and content descriptors. The five ratings include: Early Childhood, Kids to Adult, Teen, Mature, and Adults Only. ("We don't just look at violence and sexuality," Pober says; "we examine children's software from a standpoint of necessary reading and fine motor skills, such as mouse and keyboard manipulation ability, as well.") The fifteen content descriptors offer a fine breakdown of the actions and themes in the games. For instance, consumers might see phrases such as "mild animated violence," "comic mischief," "realistic blood and gore," "suggestive themes," "use of tobacco and alcohol," "use of drugs," etc.

According to Pober, this approach serves parents better than a numerical rating system. "For example, there's a big difference between passive and active violence," he comments. Active violence involves players in violent acts—destruction, murder, etc.—while passive violence involves watching events happen, as on television. While neither is desirable, active violence has more of a tendency to evoke the fight/flight response and trigger adrenaline rushes. "Our testers are trained to recognize those differences and factor them into their ratings. Besides," he continues, "even though numerical systems are used for movies, you can't simply transplant them into another medium."

As innovative and sound as ESRB's system may be, Pober is the first to admit that it doesn't eliminate the need for good parenting. He suggests that you devise your own system for what is acceptable in your household, looking at questions such as these:

• In general, does the software complement the values you're trying to teach, or negate them?

- Does the software strengthen conflict-resolution skills or demonstrate that there's no need to use them?
- Is violence built into the software? Can you play the game without getting caught up in the violent action?
- Is the software designed to make your child feel good about participating in violent actions?
- Is the level of sexuality beyond what your children are exposed to through everyday television and other media?

The bottom line, according to Pober, is that "a rating system, no matter who devises it, is just a starting point. But it's ultimately up to you to make sure that the software is used well and that it meshes with your values. Play the game yourself, and then compute with kids. By the way, that's a good idea anyway."

## Summary

Never judge a software package by the copy on the box. As you gain more experience at evaluating different genres of software, you'll adopt your own pattern of inquiry that will help you decide if a software package is worthy of your money and your children's precious time. You'll also get faster at the process and will be able to quickly separate the winners from the losers.

Chapter 7

# The Wild Wild Web

## Choosing Web Sites for Your Kids

### *A Sea of Information*

"We're studying the Titanic in school," my daughter Audrey announced at dinner. "We learned they're trying to make it float up with big balloons."

I thought it would be interesting to see what kind of related tidbits we could find on the Net, perhaps some interesting trivia she could bring to school to share with her first-grade classmates.

After helping with kitchen cleanup, we logged on to the Internet and pointed our Web browser at one of the search engines, then quickly found ourselves with a selection of more than fifty Titanic-related sites that met our criteria. Many turned out to be the equivalent of electronic souvenir kiosks or brochures for new books on the subject, but we finally struck digital pay dirt when we opened The Original Titanic Home Page. This excellent site was overflowing with photos of the ship, crew, and passengers, and provided a wealth of information relating to the construction of the vessel, lists of the provisions taken onboard for the fateful voyage, and the latest theories on why it sank.

Audrey thought that her classmates would enjoy the provisions list as well as a photo of the Titanic and her sister ships streaming through the open waters. So we printed out the appropriate pages and placed them in a "Titanic Information" folder for the next day.

The info was a hit; Audrey's teachers turned the provisions numbers into math and counting exercises that tied nicely into the study unit. (Wow—that's a long way from my first-grade education forty years ago, when Dick and Jane ruled the day and Spot's locomotion was as close as we came to science.)

Where else but the World Wide Web could you instantly collect information on the number of potatoes taken aboard the Titanic? In fact, to paraphrase the old Arlo Guthrie song, "Alice's Restaurant," you can get just about anything you want on the World Wide Web. Among other things, the Web is a combination telephone, library, shopping mall, newspaper archive, travel agency, encyclopedia, radio, and post office. It's also a place to meet people from around the world who share your interests exactly—people you would probably never connect with in any other way. And it's a communications channel that offers a gateway to a mind-numbing amount of information. It's possible to approach the Web with just about any question you can imagine, and find some sort of answer or direction. In some cases, it's a one-stop information resource; in others, it's a first-stop print- and electronic-resource locator.

Unfortunately, the quality of information and presentations is uneven. Some of the sites are well worth your viewing time; they contain excellent information presented in a compelling format. Many, however, contain scant information or present information very poorly. Others are just glitter and glitz, existing simply to demonstrate cool technology. And still others amount to little more than electronic vanity plates, the nineties version of the forties phrase "Kilroy was here."

So why bother? Because you can find some real pearls amidst the electronic flotsam and jetsam. The payoff includes information that you can't get anywhere else, and access to great libraries and archives scattered across the globe. You can gain entry to once-proprietary databases on a variety of subjects. You can also find information that simply hasn't made it into print and exists only in electronic format. And you can find cutting-edge information that's updated in a way not possible with any other medium. In short, the Web can be a very useful adjunct to your information tool kit. It can be a highly effective way to do research for home and school projects. It can be an excellent resource for finding other resources—a gateway to a world of information that at one time could be accessed only through libraries and by those with professional training. I also believe that it's worth becoming Web savvy now, because the Web is going to get better. Much of the junk will go away as the providers of frivolous sites get bored or realize that they don't have the time, incentive, or wherewithal to upload high-quality information and update it regularly.

So how do you locate sites that are worth pointing your browser toward? For that matter, how do you find anything on the Web? The rest of this chapter will help you learn about recommended sites, learn how to find sites on your own, and most important, learn how to evaluate whether a site is worth your time.

## *Finding Sites: Do Your Homework*

It seems paradoxical to search for sites when millions of them inhabit cyberspace. The trick is to find sites that are appropriate in terms of content and presentation. Here are some quick ways to start building a list of your own favorites.

## *No-Tech Approaches*

### 1. Read up.

New books and magazines on cyberspace seem to hit the shelves every week. The magazines about the Internet are usually crammed with recommendations for sites on subjects ranging from cooking and parenting to science, education, and pop culture. Key point: Mere listings of sites often aren't worth the paper they're printed on; focus on annotated listings that at least try to tell why a site is worth visiting and what's especially worth noting when you're there. While you might not ultimately agree with the annotation, you'll at least have the benefit of a report by someone who's actually visited the site and compared it with others.

Books devoted to the Internet generally fall into one of

two categories: *how-to* and *what-to*. The how-to books explain the mechanics of the Web, tips and tricks for getting the most from online sessions, etiquette for electronic communication, using search engines, and related topics. Buy one if you're new to the Web, or if you've been playing it by ear and want to fill in your knowledge gaps.

The *what-to* books are directories of selected sites that the author deems worthwhile. They range from massive tomes covering a broad range of topics from A to Z, to specific subjects such as health, sports, and pop culture.

Your newspaper is probably another good source of information about Web sites. More and more papers include reviews of worthwhile sites for businesses and families. Even local television newscasts are beginning to feature selected Web sites as a service to viewers.

## 2. Talk to friends.

Your local "parent net" gossip chain can be an excellent source of URLs (Web addresses). When people know that others are interested in worthy Web sites, they tend to exchange them on a regular basis.

## 3. Talk to teachers and technology coordinators at your kids' schools.

You're probably accustomed to asking your children's teachers for book suggestions. Ask about their favorite Web sites, too. Technology coordinators are trained to find useful things to do with the Web, and can be terrific sources of information and ideas.

## The High-Tech Approach: Using the Web to Find the Web

In addition to using media sources and your people network to locate Web sites, you can use powerful search engines and directories that the Web itself contains to make it easy to locate places to visit for browsing or for finding specific information. While it would take an entire book to do justice to the subject of searching the Internet, here's a crash course designed to help you get started.

Search engines are software programs that scour the Web to catalog and organize sites, and list them in a searchable database. The search engines themselves "live" at Web sites, and you access them by typing in a specific address (see below). The following search engines are particularly useful for locating info. Each offers a different presentation format, and you should experiment to find which best suits your search needs and your children's information needs.

AltaVista (www.altavista.digital.com)
Yahoo! (www.yahoo.com)
Infoseek (www2.Infoseek.com)
HotBot (www.hotbot.com)
Excite (www.excite.com)
Lycos (www.lycos.com)

While you'll probably settle on a favorite search tool, it's sometimes best to use a combination of tools to ensure that you have a complete sweep. Your goal should be to find the information you're seeking as quickly as possible; the less time you and your kids spend searching the Web, the more time you have to translate data into information and information into knowledge and understanding.

## Searching Techniques

Once you reach a search-engine site, you'll be presented with a screen that allows you to type in a keyword or a combination of words. You then sit back and wait for a listing of matches to your search. In theory, that's about all there is to it. In practice, though, you'll find that your search strategy can make or break your effort. Depending on what you seek, you may find as few as one site or as many as millions of sites! A lot depends on how you enter the search *query*. Here's an example of how you would use two of the popular search engines.

### AltaVista.

Let's say you want to buy a dog for your family, and you want to find breeders in your area. Type in the word *dog*, and click on the Search button. At the time of this writing, AltaVista reports 546,000 Web pages that contain information about dogs. Not terribly useful. Now, modify the search with a specific dog; say, enter "Labrador retriever." It's important to use the quotation marks so that AltaVista knows to look for both Labrador and Retriever. This time, the list is 1,000 hits. Closer, but still no bone. Now try entering "Labrador retriever" + "buying a puppy." This search finds 85 matches, through which you can sort pretty quickly to find breeders.

## Yahoo!

Yahoo! (which is actually a giant directory, not a search engine) organizes the Web into categories, such as Business, Entertainment, Recreation, and Science. Each category has subcategories to help you narrow your search. You can type in a word (or words) to search, or click on category headings until you find exactly what you want. Let's run the old dog scenario through Yahoo! and see what turns up. Start by clicking on Recreation. This displays another list. Choose Animals, Insects, and Pets, which among various subtopics includes Dogs. Click on Dogs. From here, you'll have only ten choices, including Breeds. Under Breeds, you'll find Labs. Click on this option, and you'll find a list of home pages of breeders, by region.

Both tools took you to the information you wanted, although Yahoo! got you there a little more quickly and intuitively (you could have also entered a full query in Yahoo! and ignored the organizational structure). With AltaVista, though, you'd have found useful ancillary tips, such as how to train and care for a puppy.

Experiment with AltaVista and the other search engines. You might also periodically check the Internet-related magazines for reports about new search engines. Right now the search engines are free and you can explore as you wish. So get your kids involved, too. Give them a taste for tracking down information; they'll have fun and acquire valuable skills that will pay major dividends as their homework becomes more demanding.

## Take Note!

In the process of looking for worthy sites you'll often pull up site descriptions for inappropriate or offensive sites that may contain the same words being searched. For example, when you search for toy sites you will encounter a number of "adult toy" sites that sell sexual objects. If you're concerned, you might want to take a reconnaissance run first without your kids and check out the topics that they plan to search. You can then decide whether you want them to proceed or how you'll frame your wishes concerning the undesirable materials.

Whatever source you use to find Web sites, you'll eventually develop your own criteria for deciding which ones represent a good use of your time. As with software, one person's favorite site might be at the top of another's "why bother" list. Still, certain aspects of a site, such as its ease of navigation and the credentials of its information providers, ought to be considered when you begin evaluating any particular site.

## *Three or Four Clicks and You're Out*

Imagine going to a store that required you to go to one counter to select an item, climb up six flights of stairs to pay, take an elevator down two floors and transfer to yet another elevator, and finally arrive at the subbasement where you picked up your goods. You would probably not chalk up the experience as pleasurable shopping. In fact, if you stuck it out at all, you'd likely be unwilling to return.

Similarly, few people are likely to revisit Web sites that force viewers to navigate through a labyrinthine maze or click until their fingers go numb to get to the desired information. As a rule, I think people should not have to click more than three or four times to find something useful; if they do, whoever designed the site wasn't considering the viewer as a customer.

For examples of good sites, check out Amazon.com Books (www.amazon.com), CNET—the online magazine (www.cnet.com), the CNN site (www.CNN.com), or *Time* magazine's site (www.pathfinder.com/time/). You're cooking from the moment you start clicking. San Francisco's fine Exploratorium site (www.exploratorium.com) and the Smithsonian Institution's (www.si.edu) also demonstrate how nested information can be displayed within the three- or four-click boundary.

## Good Depth = Good Surfing

The developers of solid Web sites take time to study the message they want to present, and deliver it clearly and coherently. A large problem with the Web is the "sound byte" approach to learning; some Web pundits claim that a screenful of information (about three-hundred words) is the limit. Now, there is something to be said for being concise, and there is an art form to writing good three-hundred-word chunks. But at the same time, it's impossible to do justice to many topics in such limited bursts. Look for sites that don't make you scroll through the basement, but at the same time haven't chopped up information into units so small that you lose your train of thought linking from A to B.

A useful site will strike a balance between the requirements of the medium and the nature of the subject. MSNBC (www.msnbc.com) is a good example of how a news organization gives you the best of all worlds in terms of information presentation. When you click on a news item, you'll get a capsule summary and the option to read the full story.

Your children are used to getting information from a variety of media. The Web is truly a new medium and still very much a work in progress. So as you peruse sites, consider the content presentation and depth in terms of your children's attention span, assignment needs, and abilities to extract information.

## Who's in Charge Here?

When you go to the bookstore or library to find a book that will help you make a medical choice, solve a parenting problem, choose a school, or something of equal importance, you'll no doubt base your decision on the author's credentials. It's the same with magazine articles; you're more likely to choose to spend your limited spare time reading a piece by a known expert than by someone with no experience in the field. While the print publishing world is by no means free of fools, at least it's driven by an editorial process with some filtering criteria; book and magazine publishers make an attempt to base their contract and writing assignments on the author's credentials. Also, in the publishing world, at least one pair of eyes other than the author's have reviewed and judged the materials on some level.

With the Web, there's little accountability. Anyone who has access to the Net is potentially a publisher. Software exists that makes it a breeze for anyone to put up a Web page for the world to see. While this may have a certain democratic appeal, and it does open the doors of electronic publishing, it also means that you have to be particularly discriminating when you choose information sources for your children and yourself.

Some sites are sponsored by a national organization, government agency, or educational institution. With these, you at least know the information source and can deduce its quality. But if you don't see a name that rings a bell or credentials that you trust (or see a name at all), treat the information with caution. It may or may not be accurate. Just remember that when it comes to the accuracy and authenticity of information on the Web, you're flying by the seat of your pants.

## Caveat Viewer

Unless you've gotten a Web site recommendation from a friend, teacher, or other trusted source, give prospective candidates for your children's viewing a good look before you put them on your *approved* list. You can't learn anything about a site from the title alone or from a description provided by a search engine; sometimes the most seemingly innocent sites have a few surprises in store. Note the links to other sites, too, and follow them. Just as you'd never judge a book by its cover or a software program by its box, don't judge a Web site on the basis of its front page. So spend a little time exploring a site before you can endorse it. The old saw "Better safe than sorry" is tailor-made for the Web.

## *Summary*

The Web is teeming with sites that run the gamut from informative to vacuous and, to borrow from the motion picture industry, from PG level to X rated. Read up, look up, then check up on prospective sites for your kids. And by the way, have fun; the Web is slowly turning into a mainstream way for you to get news, shop, research information, and entertain yourself. Besides, your kids will admire you for being a techno-savvy, plugged-in parent!

# Chapter 8

# From Cyberspace to Your Space

## Connecting with Your Kids at the Keyboard

### *Getting Back to Basics*

During an airplane jaunt from New York to Boston, I struck up a conversation with the passenger sitting next to me. He had kids close in age to mine and with similar interests in soccer, so we hit it off immediately. When I told him that I'd co-authored a book on TV-free activities with my wife, his eyes lit up and he exclaimed, "Oh, the chubby little white book—we use it all the time! When are you going to write a book about computer-free activities? It's getting harder and harder to tear them away from the PC and just have fun the way we used to when they were little."

I was pleased that he knew of our book, and told him that I had no plans for such a sequel. Instead, I suggested various activities he could do with his kids *and* his computer. "It's like replacing cardboard tubes with a smart electronic tube," I said. "The idea is to just find a medium that gives you the opportunity to connect with your kids and share some good times."

That struck a chord; we yearn to connect or reconnect with our kids, especially as we see all the pressures they face to grow up too soon. But how can we keep up with our kids' incredible technological prowess and, better yet, add value to their experience with the computer? By getting involved early and intensively, and introducing the one thing that no hardware or software can offer your children: your interest, respect, and encouragement. Whatever normal friction you have with your children, you're still the person who can leap tall buildings and set the world aright.

As corny as this idea may sound, I think it rings true for many parents. It also explains the success of my little book of TV-free activities. While I'm proud of the book's popularity, I'm the first to admit that it doesn't break new ground in the history of human ideas. In fact, the book is very simple and teaches people (or refreshes their memory about) how to have good old-fashioned fun with simple role-playing games and activities involving cardboard tubes, recycled packaging materials, and common household items.

The power of this simple approach became evident to me one night when I was asked to present activity ideas to a group of parents in a community that was planning a three-day TV turnoff. Some people objected to the turnoff because they didn't like being told what to do in their own living rooms. But others were concerned about what they'd do during the "days of darkness," as one parent described it. For my talk, I brought in my standard bag of stuff: cardboard tubes, recycled paper plates and cups, string, tennis balls, empty milk jugs, and other goodies. As I set up my props for the demo, I noticed that the kids were of the twelve- to fourteen-year-old variety, not the six- to eight-year-olds I was accustomed to entertaining. "They're going to string me from the rafters," I moaned to myself, wondering how you entertain preteens with a bag of trash.

To my delight, and the parents' utter shock, we had a blast. We played toilet-tube bowling. We put on a skit with alien masks we'd created out of paper bags. We invented memory games. We put on our mock TV show using paper-bag TV helmets. No one uttered a single dis or hiss the entire time. The only complaint from the kids was that we had to leave because our allotted time at the school was up. Clearly, they just enjoyed having an adult spend unconditional time with them; I acted as a goofy peer, not as an instructor.

The parents at this meeting unanimously decided they'd go ahead with the turnoff, not so much because they thought it would change their kids' TV-watching behaviors, but because they saw an opportunity to reconnect with their kids away from the television set.

I see the same potential with computer technology. You can connect with your kids by talking about hardware specs and the latest games. But you can also connect by taking an active role in designing projects for them to do. You can be the family funmeister, as well as a participant in the projects, too.

This chapter gives you some starter activity ideas for using computer technology that you already likely own to reinforce your children's basic skills, expand their communication abilities, and use the computer in new ways. The first part covers ideas for using your existing software (word processors, graphics programs, electronic encyclopedias, and children's storybook software). The second section covers online learning adventures you can lead right from your own living room.

## *Software Activities*

**CATEGORY: Electronic Reference Programs**
**ACTIVITY:** Digital Fact Finders
**CONCEPT:** Each day, your kids use an electronic reference source to find the following:

- an interesting fact (for example, the whale shark is the largest of all sharks, sixty feet long but harmless to humans)
- a memorable date (such as the birth of a famous poet or the signing of a treaty)
- a description of an event (perhaps a volcanic eruption such as Krakatoa or Mount St. Helens)
- a principle (maybe the Bernoulli principle, which accounts for the lift of airplane wings) or a theory (such as what caused the disappearance of the dinosaurs)
- geographical facts (populations, natural resources, etc.)

For starters, you can leave the categories open and ask family members to search an electronic encyclopedia or a reference compendium for something that catches their fancy. This tactic encourages aimless browsing rather than targeted searching, opening the door for serendipitous discovery. Whatever they find, family members can present the information during dinner or at some appointed time during the day. Alternatively, you can state a category for people to research, such as science, history, or geography. For older kids, you can make the category more specific, such as American history, physics, geology, Far Eastern culture, etc.

Tips for making the activities work:

1. Take turns. Each day, let a different family member assign a category or decide what is to be found (a date, place, etc.).
2. Provide a good forum for each person to give his or her presentation. Perhaps each person is allowed up to three minutes to speak without interruption, then others can ask questions.
3. Make sure each participant has equal (or enough) time at the computer.

CATEGORY: **Electronic Reference Programs**
ACTIVITY: Reference Desk
CONCEPT: Your child acts as reference librarian for other members of the household. You submit a request for a topic to be researched, and your child presents a report verbally or in writing. Tailor the subject matter to match your "librarian's" interests and skill levels. You might ask your junior reference expert to research topics such as the following:

• When was the first presidential election held in the United States, and what were the events that led up to it?

- What is the largest dinosaur known to humans, and how did it live?
- How is coal formed?
- Who was the first astronaut to walk on the moon, and what else happened on his mission?
- Why do people need to sleep, and what happens if they don't?
- Where was the first public school established in this country, and who attended it?

Tips for making the activities work:

1. Guide your child through the process of electronic fact-finding until he or she feels comfortable going it alone.
2. Be available to answer your child's questions as they arise.
3. Take the opportunity to learn from your child. When he or she finds the information you requested, be sure to say, "I'm very impressed; how did you ever find that?"
4. Encourage your child to illustrate the reports using electronic paint tools or traditional media.

CATEGORY: **Word Processing/Desktop Publishing**
ACTIVITY: Media Machine
CONCEPT: You and your kids create original publications to share with each other, and with friends and relatives. To begin, gather magazines, brochures, and other print materials from around the house to use as models. Encourage participants to improve upon these samples (and on the program's built-in templates) through experimentation. Here are some starter project ideas:

- a neighborhood gazette that presents all the community news that's fit to print
- a travel brochure that encourages readers to visit your hometown
- a newsletter that highlights a recent family vacation
- a flyer that announces a backyard barbecue, a family theater show, or another event to which friends, neighbors, and relatives are invited

Tips for making the activities work:

1. Designate an editor (on a rotating basis) who assigns each family member articles, stories, or paragraphs. Give each writer, or illustrator, a byline.
2. Photocopy the publication, and send (or give) the duplicates to friends, family, and "subscribers." Encourage readers to contribute articles, too.
3. Keep a dated file of hard-copy originals for your family library.

CATEGORY: **Word Processing/Desktop Publishing**
ACTIVITY: Creative Communications
CONCEPT: Assign your kids topics and genres, and encourage them to experiment with fonts, spacing, color, size, and other word-processing/desktop-publishing design elements to enhance their writings. Here are some activities to suggest:

- Create a poem with a message that uses only one word, such as the name of a fruit, a pet, a season, or a sport.

The poet uses spacing, bold type, italics, capital letters, colors, etc., to convey the mood. For instance, the word *volume* might be typed in increasingly large type sizes and intensifying colors to convey the sense of escalating loudness.

- Write a persuasive editorial on an important topic like recycling, volunteering, or bicycle safety.
- Write a science fiction story that takes place on a distant planet or in another century.
- Produce advertisements for an environmentally correct breakfast cereal, junk food, or a favorite toy or computer game.

Tips for making the activities work:

1. Print out enough copies so that everyone in the family has one.
2. Encourage writers to read their work aloud—uninterrupted—at a family forum.
3. After each reading, have an ideas exchange during which participants offer both positive criticism (that should always come first!) and editorial suggestions.
4. Let family members take turns coming up with creative writing assignments.

CATEGORY: **Word Processing/Desktop Publishing**
ACTIVITY: Language Games
CONCEPT: Family members use word processing/desktop publishing programs to create fun and challenging exercises such as the following:

• Create a code in which a character is substituted for each letter of the alphabet (for example, ! for "a," @ for "b," % for "c," etc.). Give family members a copy of the key, which they can use to encrypt and decode messages.

• Type a short story or poem, substituting an asterisk (*), or wildcard character, for key nouns (for example, "A young * attended a * with a * . . ."). Each participant, using the master document, searches for the asterisks, fills in his or her choices for each, then saves the document under a new name so that each participant has a custom version of the original document. When everyone is finished, read the silly stories or poems aloud.

• Make a search puzzle with a theme such as holidays, cities, foods, and so on. Type twenty words vertically, horizontally, backward, and forward (increase or decrease the number of words according to players' ages and skills). Then add nonsense letters around them to create a rectangle of letters. Save the puzzle, then print out copies for family members. Ask them to circle all the hidden words.

• Try some captioneering. Ask your kids to write and print out captions, then affix them to photos from the newspaper, magazines, or junk mail. After dinner or during a family night, pass out the zany caption-photo combinations for some good laughs.

Tips for making the activities work:

1. Discourage competition among family members in favor of having them work together to find the answers or beat their own personal best.
2. Encourage creativity and experimentation. For exam-

ple, kids can use clip art or borders to decorate puzzles or stories.

3. Let participants devise their own game rules and variations for each round; invention is half the fun!

CATEGORY: **Storybook Software (younger kids)**
ACTIVITY: Chain Stories
CONCEPT: Choose a favorite electronic story with your children (this is a great way to extend the shelf life of books on plastic). You and your kids take turns adding one or two lines at a time to create chain stories retelling the software tales in novel ways that get the kids to think about the characters, plots, and other tale components so they can extend these elements and exercise their storymaking skills.

• Add additional characters. Retell the tale, incorporating the new characters (which can be people, animals, or mythical beings), and see how the story changes. Perhaps the new characters teach positive lessons or create comical subplots for scary tales.

• Move the story to another country or time period. Encourage family members to use reference resources (such as CDs, encyclopedias, and atlases) to learn details that will add realism to the characters and plots.

• Add a new chapter to tell a story that begins after the CD's tale ends. Family members take turns contributing an epilogue, perhaps using a paint program like KidPix to create scenes and characters.

• Tell the story backwards. Begin at the ending, continue with the middle, and work your way to the beginning.

• Turn a minor character into the hero of the tale. See whether you can fully develop the minor character so well that he or she eclipses the old protagonist.

To get the ball rolling, you might want to begin the story with a paragraph or two. If younger storytellers get stuck at some point, you or another participant can fill in a few lines to keep the plot moving ahead.

Tips for making the activities work:

1. Refresh everyone's memory before you begin by retelling the storybook CD's plot. Perhaps summarize the scenes or main points.
2. Set a time limit. You're the best expert on your child, so you know when the activity will begin to wear thin.
3. Set the ground rules in advance, such as "No interrupting storytellers when it's their turn," "Each person gets sixty seconds to speak," "We decide the sequence of storytellers by picking names from a hat," etc.
4. Supply a tape recorder or video camera to capture your family members' chain-story sessions.
5. Ask a family scribe to write (or word process) the new tales, and add them to a Stories Journal, perhaps using a paint program to add illustrations.
6. When you've finished a tale, compare your family's version with the original.

CATEGORY: **Storybook Software (younger kids)**
ACTIVITY: Family Theater Night
CONCEPT: Each family member chooses a storybook charac-

ter to role-play (choose names from a hat or have a casting director assign parts). Then, stage the following types of shows:

- Family members create their own costumes, props, sets, and so on, and then improvise dialogue, which can be based on the storybook's plot.
- Role-play the same characters, but improvise a sequel, a prequel or a different ending to the original tale.
- Before the show, each person draws two character names from two hats. Stage the tale, with each participant role-playing his or her first character. Then, when the designated director calls "Switch," resume the show with each actor portraying the second character.
- Choose roles by picking names from a hat. Actors have a predetermined amount of time (say, five, ten, or fifteen minutes, depending on your children's ages and skills) to prepare a brief monologue based on the storybook CD.
- As in the previous example, the actors perform monologues one at a time. In this variation, however, audience members try to guess which character is speaking.
- Mix and match characters from several storybooks to create a new stage show.
- Turn the storybook tale into an opera, ballet, or pantomime.

Keep a "wardrobe-and-props trunk" handy (a box that your kids decorate and fill with cast-off clothes, hats, recycled plastic and paper goods, and the like). Hold a rehearsal or two, with older siblings or a director suggesting lines for younger kids. Then, when the players feel comfortable in their roles, stage the show, complete with costumes and props. If you have a willing cameraperson available, consider videotaping the production.

Tips for making the activities work:

1. Make sure everyone has a stint at being the director (perhaps each family member keeps the job title for one show, or for one Family Theater Night).
2. Rotate the "important" roles so everyone, in turn, can be a star.
3. When possible, invite friends, relatives, and other "patrons" to watch, and perhaps join the show.
4. Compare family members' interpretations of characters, and talk about how each performance changes the story.
5. Extend the play by creating simple jobs for little kids, such as costume designer, wardrobe manager, etc.

CATEGORY: **Storybook Software (younger kids)**
ACTIVITY: **From CD to Paper**
CONCEPT: Use the electronic storybook as a springboard for creating original text and artwork. Your kids develop their writing, drawing, and storytelling talents as they enjoy their favorite storybook CDs.

- Create a traditional storybook based on a CD. Each family member writes and illustrates a complete book, or each person contributes a page.
- Family novelists create a storybook based on the question "And then what happened?" or "What would have happened if . . ."

- Publish a biography or diary of a favorite character.
- Write and illustrate storybooks by combining characters, and perhaps plots, from several favorite CDs.
- Take the story from the CD and place it against the backdrop of a historical event.
- Turn your favorite CD storybook into a comic book.

Use word processors and/or art programs with color printers; or try a traditional story-making method such as three-holed paper and a loose-leaf binder, a note pad or drawing tablet, or drawing paper stapled or clipped together.

Tips for making the activities work:

1. Create cover pages for your books, including titles, authors, illustrators, and dates.
2. Have older kids or adults act as scribes for younger siblings; alternatively, preschoolers can illustrate others' text.
3. Encourage family writers and artists to use their imaginations, and not to worry about sticking to the original tale.

CATEGORY: **Paint/Draw/Graphics Programs**
ACTIVITY: Bright Ideas
CONCEPT: Encourage your kids to use a graphics or paint program to bring their visions, creations, and ideas to the computer screen, and then print them out to share with friends and relatives.

- Graphically represent an idea, fact, or historical event. The graphic representation might be a flow chart that shows sequential processes, or nested boxes and circles that show orders of magnitude (such as the progression from home address to town, to county, to city, all the way up to a planetary level), or an organizational chart that depicts hierarchical relationships, such as the structure of the federal government.

- Create an invention, using the various shape tools and special effects functions. Then let everyone try to guess what the invention does.

- Capture a dream or waking image on screen. Focus on re-creating the mood, rather than conveying tangible objects and people. (Suggest that young kids use the erase tool to get the better of their nightmare monsters.)

- Draw an X-ray version of a common machine or appliance, depicting the gears, wires, and other gizmos that make the item work. Kids can create pictures from their imaginations, or research actual objects to produce real-life diagrams.

- Create composite animals (mixed heads, torsos, etc.) that can reside only in the imagination. For each fanciful animal, your children should explain what part of the world (or galaxy) it would live in, what it would eat, and what its care and feeding instructions would be (if the critter could be domesticated).

Tips for making the activities work:

1. Recommend that your artists begin with simple representations, such as the events of a typical day in their

lives. As your kids get the hang of it, suggest pictorial representations for the plot of a book, biological processes like photosynthesis, or the division of government.

2. Suggest that color can also be a means of organizing and highlighting key information; encourage experimentation with the use of color to convey emphasis and ideas.

3. Explain to your kids that there's no right or wrong in drawing; their artistic renderings are as valid as anyone else's.

CATEGORY: **Paint/Draw/Graphics Programs**
ACTIVITY: Design Masters
CONCEPT: Create items that identify your family (or community) to the rest of the world and make a lasting impression on friends and relatives.

- Design a family logo, with a tag line that captures the spirit of your household (for example, "The family that loves the outdoors," with a logo depicting trees and mountains). Use it on the family brochure, stationery, newsletter, or other publications described earlier.

- Create a coat of arms that reflects your family's heritage.

- Design a flag for your family, street, neighborhood, city, or state. Or perhaps one for a unified planet earth that could be used on a spacecraft.

- Create team T-shirts or hats for family members or friends. Later, you can transfer the artwork to real-life clothing items by using iron-on transfer paper designed for ink-jet printers, if you so desire.

Tips for making the activities work:

1. If you don't have a color printer, print on plain paper and have your children use crayons, paint, markers, and other readily available media.
2. See whether participants can create communal art projects, and work together to create a unified family expression.
3. When designing various logos, coats of arms, flags, or clothes, keep in mind the many sides to your family: fun, serious, silly, and the like. A design might commemorate a family vacation, a concern for the environment, an interest in sports, and so on.

**CATEGORY: Paint/Draw/Graphics Programs**
**ACTIVITY: Game Designers**
**CONCEPT:** Children never tire of games they create themselves. Here are a bunch of original low-cost play items they can create with the computer:

- Game boards. Create playing boards with a paint or drawing program. You can make these by copying squares and other shapes, or by simply making a winding path of geometric shapes. Then, supply dice and playing pieces (cardboard squares, checkers, etc.), and suggest that your kids make up the rules for moving the pieces, for the goals of the game, and so on.
- Playing cards. There's no reason why your kids have to stick to the same old four suits; why not make theme cards

(including, say, an ace of vegetables, a two of fruit, a three of grains, a four of protein, etc.).

- Targets. These are cardboard boxes onto which your kids glue computer-generated artwork to indicate their point values. Players can toss balls or beanbags into them and rack up high (or low, depending on the rules) scores.
- Animal or other posters. Kids can play their own version of Pin the Tail on the Donkey by hanging their poster on the wall and, with eyes closed, using double-stick tape to adhere homemade tails to the drawing.

Tips for making the activities work:

1. When kids play for points, encourage them to exceed their last scores rather than outpace their competitors. Often, de-emphasizing the competitive aspects of family games leads to a more enjoyable time (for instance, have people contribute to a grand total and see if the family can better its prior score).
2. If games must have a winner, let that person choose the rules for the next round of play. Again, this takes some of the focus off winning for its own sake and places the emphasis on moving on to the next game.
3. Create a family games journal, and keep track of family favorites as well as players' personal records.

CATEGORY: **Image-editing/Digital Photography**
ACTIVITY: Digital Creativity Lab
CONCEPT: Family members use image-editing software and digital cameras (still and video) to create fun and exciting

projects and games. The software can be used to juxtapose elements of different photographs, add wild features (through morphing programs), and integrate photographs with text and other graphic elements. The following kinds of projects will place photography in a whole new light.

- Use digital-imaging tools to create your own labels for everything from soup cans and soda bottles to gift boxes and tissue boxes. Affix the labels with double-stick tape or glue. This activity also lends itself nicely to parties and other occasions where zaniness is a plus.
- Make intriguing masks by affixing home-produced photos to a paper bag, then cutting out holes for the eyes, nose, and mouth. The photos might be the faces of friends, family members, or even the household pet. You can create offbeat masks by using portions of photos to create various facial features. For instance, a food mask might consist of the following elements trimmed from photos: a slice of melon for a mouth, an egg for the nose, kiwi slices for the eyes, and for the hair—angel hair pasta!
- Make a hand puppet by affixing a photo to the closed end of a sock (use double-stick tape). The picture might be of a family member, a pet, a household object, or a composite of various images. You can also affix photo cutouts to plastic cutlery to make stick puppets. Hold the handles of the puppets at the edge of a table, and you're ready to put on a great performance.
- Use stills or videos to produce a demo. The demo might be of something technical, like building a model, creating a particular type of arts and crafts project, or perhaps of how to make a favorite meal (like peanut butter and

jelly sandwiches). If you have a still camera, use a sequence of photos and text (merge them with a word processor or page-layout program) to explain what's going on. If you have a digital video camera, you can record the sequence or portions of it. Perhaps hold a "film festival" demonstrating a variety of projects and artistic approaches.

• Create a family newscast. If you have a digital video camera, you can use it to keep your "wired" distant relatives and friends informed. Take turns being the news "anchor" and report on important events happening in your household, at school, or in the neighborhood. Your kids will enjoy the opportunity to be "on air" and your friends and relatives will enjoy this high-tech way of staying in touch.

Tips for making the activities work:

1. Encourage the spirit of experimentation; after all, one of the beauties of digital imaging is that you can create endlessly without incurring any film processing costs.
2. Stress the fact that there is no "right" or correct way to do any of the projects; the idea is to extend the traditional notion of photography.
3. Make sure you have all the additional materials you'll need ahead of time—glue or double-stick tape, cardboard, straws, etc. You don't want to break the creative flow by having to hunt for supplies.

## *Web-Based Activities*

The Web also offers great opportunities to create *info hunts* and Internet *field trips* that will not only provide good information about a variety of topics, but will help you and your children become more Web savvy. Caution: Whenever you create games or field trips, think twice before turning your children loose in cyberspace; at least be there as a silent partner or use a content-filtering program to block out inappropriate materials (see the Appendix for a list of such software packages).

### Creating Games on the Web

If you enjoy putting together scavenger or treasure hunts for your kids' birthday parties, you'll find that the Web affords you the opportunity to create intriguing variations on an old theme. Instead of looking for clues hidden among furniture or other objects, your treasure hunters search the Web for virtual clues that will take them to their destinations. You'll become quite proficient at using search engines by putting together the hunts. Your kids will enjoy a bit of at-home learning, and best of all, will appreciate the fact that you created the games. The following sections describe a simple process for creating Web games for your children.

### Search-and-Find Games

Here's a basic blueprint for putting together a find-it game based on the Web.

1. Pick a theme. Remember, the Web has information on just about anything—dinosaurs, capital cities, flags, the history of chocolate, etc. For younger children, you might want to do something about animals; for older children, you might choose, say, space, sports, music, or history as a theme.

2. Use your favorite search engine to find a handful of Web sites that pertain to your theme. Here's where a directory like Yahoo! (www.yahoo.com) comes in handy. (See Chapter 7.) You can click through Yahoo!'s subcategories to find sites on your topic.

3. Spend a few minutes navigating through the sites you've chosen. Try to pick sites with plenty of information and vivid graphics. Also, it's easier for children to discover new facts if the site is well organized and presents information and resources clearly.

4. If your children are older, you can list each site's URL (address) on a sheet of paper for them to type in themselves. For younger kids, you might want to add the sites to your browser's bookmarks or list of favorite places, so it will be easy for them to get from one site to the next.

5. Write down questions to answer or objects to find for each site. Perhaps ask for a genus and species of a particular critter for the animal activity, or the gravitational strength of various planets for the space activity. Make sure you jot down the answers (and keep them hidden), as well as any hints to finding them, in case some answers are too difficult to obtain.

Let the fun begin!

## Digital Field Trips

Another way to introduce children to Web sites and new people and places is to create electronic field trips that tie together a group of thematically related sites. Use a search engine to pick out sites on a particular topic, such as history, music, space, math, etc., then select five or six complementary sites that fit together nicely when visited sequentially during a twenty- or thirty-minute viewing. The goal is not to explore every nook and cranny of the sites, but to convey information about a subject using the Web's resources. Later, you and your child can return to the sites and explore them individually in more depth.

Let's say that you want to use the Web to give your kids a preview of the government buildings in Washington, D.C. After using one or more of the basic search engines, you'd wind up with an impressive list of government-related sites. You might then winnow down the field trip to a set of sites that covers the most common (and impressive) elements of our capitol.

Why not start with the most executive of all government edifices—the White House? How would you like to see democracy at work? The Internet makes it possible to take a virtual tour of the White House (www.whitehouse.gov) during which you can "meet" the president and vice president; that is, you can learn about their accomplishments and their families, and even communicate with them via e-mail. If you have younger children, you might want to start with the White House for Kids section, where Socks, the Clintons' cat, acts as a personal guide on a tour tailored especially for the young visitors.

Next, you might suggest stopping at the Washington Monument Virtual Visitors Center (www.nps.gov/wamo/index2.htm). There, you can see the Washington Monument at sunrise via a stunning photo; discover the surprising history of the Monument; and find links to Constitution Gardens, Ford's Theatre, the Lincoln Memorial, the Vietnam Veterans Memorial, and other historical locales.

You'll also want to put the United States Capitol (www.aoc.gov/) on your must-see list, of course. Besides learning about the Capitol's architects, you can visit its historic rooms, enjoy its art collection, and even stroll around its grounds. You'll also find interesting information about the Capitol Dome and Rotunda, the Old Senate Chamber, the National Sanctuary Hall, and more.

Next stop: Try the Library of Congress site (www.loc.gov) to take a peek at some of its treasures, such as George Washington's papers, abstracts of laws from foreign countries, and Congressional records that are updated at least every forty-eight hours. You can also point out a number of excellent exhibits that cover a variety of topics in American history.

In addition to increasing your children's general knowledge base, the idea of this or any other online field trip is to integrate what you've seen and learned into your kids' study units, and into events taking place in your own household, backyard, or community. After logging off, for example, use the field trip as a stimulus for discussing the democratic process (including why we can't afford to take it for granted). Perhaps you and your kids can do a bit of local research, then design and test a real field trip downtown. That's really putting the Web to work as you complete the loop by helping your children move from cyberspace to your own place.

# Summary

Traditional activities and high technology can work hand in hand. This is a worthwhile message to pass on to your children and to put into practice yourself. It means finding some extra time to get involved and a commitment to do a little preparation. But that's a pretty small price to pay for the opportunity to stay connected to your kids in today's digital world.

# Chapter 9

# The Plugged-in Parent

## Creating an Operating System for Your Household

### *Meeting Your PC Head On*

When my children were little it was easy to get them off the computer: simply bake some fresh chocolate-chip cookies and let the aroma waft through the family room. But the stomach isn't a royal road to their hearts and minds anymore.

As computers evolve, it will become increasingly difficult to offer alternatives. The real challenge may be keeping your whole family from getting lost in the machine. Consider new technologies like DVD—CD-ROM disks that contain entire full-length movies with sound tracks. The picture quality is astounding, and it's easy to imagine a situation in which whole families hunker down around a monitor. The mid-nineties even saw the introduction to the consumer market of jumbo-screen monitors for computers; several units allow family members to control the device with a re-mote controller as well as from the keyboard.

Some pundits hailed the big-screen PC as the real break-through in the home computing revolution—PC comput-ing for the whole family. To me, the jumbo-screen PC is the PC from hell. If the thought of isolated individuals com-muning with their monitors is disconcerting, the thought of a whole family staring at a monster-sized screen is truly hor-rifying. While Junior plunks at the keyboard, noodles with the mouse, or wildly thrashes the joy stick, Mom, Dad, and Sis sit entranced by the fast action on the screen. Perhaps they actually tune into some quality software and have a good time of it. But once again, here they are, sitting around the new electronic hearth and giving their minds to the machine. Once again, they become passive viewers of a medium that offers real possibilities for learning and enter-tainment. In short, they're watching television again!

Whether you own a wall-sized monster or a diminutive subnotebook computer, it's important to recognize the role we can all play in making sure that, in a decade, we're not wondering how to disentangle PCs from our kids' lives as we do about television today. In this chapter, I provide a frame-work for regulating computer use in the home that's adapted from the program I presented in *Kick the TV Habit*, a step-by-step guide for curbing television watching. While that program was obviously devoted to television watching, its crossover into computers is striking. Computers have graced our living rooms for just a few years, and already mental health experts are finding that computer addiction is a potential problem as we migrate from the TV to the PC. We have a chance now to set good examples for our kids, demonstrate our commitment to making the most out of the technology, and help our kids to regulate their own PC usage.

## Be There Now!

Throughout this book, I've talked about the necessity of being involved with your children's computing. But how can you really do that, given your busy schedule? The good news is that there's a spectrum of involvement, and you need to find a comfortable position on it for yourself. As with setting good TV-watching habits, your time should be front-end loaded. That is, the younger your child, the more time you should try to devote to establishing good computing habits. The early years are the best time to teach your child to self-regulate; as your kids get older, their computing styles and habits will likely be hard to change. Here is a range of involvement levels:

### Ideal Involvement

If you had time to spare, you would be committed to spending whatever time were necessary to learn about the technology that occupies so much of your children's time. Specifically, you would do the following:

• You would learn the basic issues about kids and computers (see Chapter 3), and set limits in terms of the amount of time your children spend on the machine each day (more on this below). You would extend your parenting prerogatives into the world of the computer, discussing appropriate use for the machine, and what type of content is appropriate for exploring or viewing during online and cyberspace explorations.

• You would make time to research potential new software purchases (either ones that you've discussed or that your kids have asked for). You'd read reviews in current computer magazines, talk to friends who own the software, and make an effort to try the programs before buying them. Then you'd install the software, and become familiar with it before your kids do.

• You would monitor the computer so you'd know what's on it in the way of programs and content.

• You would explore cyberspace yourself, surf the Web, check out an online service, send e-mail, familiarize yourself with the happenings in chat rooms, post messages, and join online discussions.

• You would reserve specific time to co-compute; that is, time when you could show your child the cool stuff you've learned. During these sessions, you'd ask your child to show you something that he or she had learned recently, and you would strive to make your child feel good about his or her mastery of the machine.

• You would closely monitor how much time your kids (and adults in the house, including yourself) spend on the computer, making sure no one was showing signs of being hooked or losing other interests.

## *Medium Involvement*

Few of us have time for ideal involvement with our children's computing. Yet even with a hectic schedule, it makes sense to try to achieve a moderate level of proficiency with the machine and to learn what you need to make good choices for your family. The medium involvement level entails the following practices:

- Learn the basics and familiarize yourself with the general landscape of cyberspace, even if you don't become a computer expert or spend much time in front of the computer.
- Set limits; establish ground rules for using the computer (based on what works best for your family members), and discuss the kind of content that's acceptable for viewing or venturing into while taking cyberspace and online jaunts.
- Let your kids tell you what kinds of software they want to buy, and try before you buy, even if you don't have time to do extensive research beforehand.
- Keep up with how software dollars are being spent, and carefully decide what will go into your family software library.
- Know what's on your computer's hard disk.
- Ensure that computing doesn't absorb a disproportionate share of any family member's time and energy. Also, watch for signs of frustration or boredom with software, and strive to keep family members productive and pleasantly challenged with computing.

## Minimum Involvement

Your schedule may be so demanding that you have very little time to spend with your children's computing. But for the reasons discussed in the preceding chapters, it's critical that you have at least a basic familiarity with the issues and attempt the following:

- Set limits and establish ground rules.
- Monitor what kind of software comes into your house.
- Stay open to signals from your family members that the computer is becoming more than just a tool; you'll know when to cut back on your child's computing time, shift into different kinds of software packages, or suggest ways in which family members can go beyond computing and use "real world" resources.

Don't feel bad if you find yourself at the minimal end of the spectrum; just making an effort to learn about the technology and the parenting issues surrounding it is a great step. Chances are, the more time you spend actually using the computer, the more you'll want to get involved with your children's screen time. Start today!

## Become a PC Role Model

Experts agree that modeling is an important part of shaping children's use and abuse of electronic media. The bottom line is that you can't expect your children to develop positive computing attitudes and behaviors unless you demonstrate them yourself. Let's go back to the television model again. If you want your kids to alter their television-watching habits, you need to change your own. If your kids are used to seeing you use the television as white noise while you cook, clean, pay bills, etc., you're communicating a strong message—namely, that the television is life-support technology. If your kids see you dash off to watch a favorite program, you're also communicating the message that it's OK to have your schedule and your life revolve around a machine.

Likewise, your kids, with their incredibly sharp powers of observation, will pick up on your computer habits and translate them into approved rules to live by. What's your computing style? See if any of the following describe your behavior:

## The Not-So-Secret Gamer

Do you ever find yourself determined to beat a game, no matter how unsatisfying or trivial the concept? Do you tell yourself that you'll spend only a minute playing, but know you'll probably be at it for at least an hour?

## The Multitasker

Do you type away quietly when you're talking to someone on the phone (hoping they won't hear the clicks and be offended), or talk to other family members while you keep pecking at the keyboard?

## The Fiddler

Do you habitually adjust screen colors or play with settings in various programs at the expense of work? Do you find that many of your experiments and explorations yield no positive improvement in the functioning and efficiency of your computing?

## The Computer Potato

Do you veg out in front of the monitor to unwind after a hard day, much the same way as you might in front of the television screen? Is the computer already turning into a replacement for television in your life, with passive and limitless viewing the order of the day?

If any of the preceding characterize your computing style, think about the message you're broadcasting to your kids. If you choose to spend a good percentage of your free time at the screen, you've made a strong statement. And if your kids know that you're determined to crack a game, then you've bolstered the idea that doing so is a worthy cause.

I know the downside of this one from personal experience. Here's what happened. After being asked to give a school lecture on computer games that reward players for destructive actions, I went to my local software store and purchased Rebel Assault (a game based on *Star Wars*). I also figured that I'd better get proficient at the game, so I could give a good demonstration of how a shoot-'em-up program works. I suddenly found myself using it more every day, just to get a "little bit better." The program is cleverly designed to help you hone your flying and shooting skills as you progress through the levels.

My hard work paid off, I suppose, as I advanced to level six. A store clerk told me the cheat codes (which allow you to undo any damage you've sustained from the Empire), and in a half hour I cheated my way to level ten and blew up the Death Star. Meanwhile, my son wanted to get in on the act, too, and it was hard for me to say no to him while I was saying yes to myself, despite my legitimate "professional" needs. It took another couple weeks before we could finally wean ourselves off the program (I passed along the cheat codes to accelerate his victory in the hopes of diminishing his interest in the program).

Like excessive game playing, multitasking at the keyboard sends a strong message to your kids. It basically says that the computer show must go on, no matter what. It also tacitly implies a subtle priority or selection process in which you decide who's worthy of your full attention and who isn't. In fact, constant attendance at the keyboard while you are doing other things can even suggest that few things, if anything, are worth our complete concentration; just about everything can be trivialized or consigned to a back burner while something flashier is happening in the computer foreground.

## *Take Stock of Your Children's Computing Habits*

Once you've gotten your own computing act together, you'll need to know what your kids actually do on the machine. As I've stressed throughout this book, don't assume that just because your kids are sitting at the keyboard, they're actually getting anything useful out of it. It's therefore important to know how much time they're spending on the machine during a typical week, and what they are doing while at the computer. There are several ways you can go about doing this:

First, there's the honor system. Create a time sheet for entering logon and logoff times, brief descriptions of what programs were used, what online activities were done, etc. Request that all household members fill out a time sheet when they power on or log off during the assessment period. For prereaders, make it a rule that they don't power on without your signing them up. Of course, you ought to fill out the time sheet, too; remember—you're the role model.

As a variant on the preceding, your kids must request permission to use the machine, so you can keep track of time while you're assessing what they're doing with the machine. You can jot down the times and observe what activities they're doing. Be careful with this approach; it can come off as punitive or invasive, as in, "the PC police are watching."

Last, there's the bits-and-bytes approach. A number of software packages will actually track the amount of time users spend on the machine, and record the programs loaded and Web sites visited (some of the packages listed in the Appendix, such as CyberPatrol, will do this). While these programs make the tracking simple, they also represent a high-tech approach to resolving a no-tech parenting issue. In addition, they suggest that you don't trust your kids. Nonetheless, if used openly and with the explanation that you're automating the tracking process for the sake of convenience and efficiency, they might prove useful in your household.

Whatever approach you take, go easy. If you meet resistance or encounter an irregular week in terms of computer usage, schedule another assessment period. And be sure to choose typical weeks; time checks done during holidays may not yield useful results, because the computer may be used more or less often (depending on whether your kids use the computer more often for entertainment or homework) than during any other week. Once you know what's going on, you can go about drawing boundaries in terms of time and content.

## *Know Thy Computer's Hard Disk*

To paraphrase a famous comedian, kids download the darndest programs. They'll also bring home the darndest things they've downloaded from friends' computers. So don't assume that the only software programs on your PC are the ones that came installed with it or ones you installed yourself. It's wise to check your computer periodically to see what your kids have been adding to the hard drive in the way of games and images.

## A Word About Privacy

Bear in mind that the act of checking your child's entries on the computer has serious privacy implications, especially where older children are involved. How comfortable are you with reading through your children's directories or folders and reading their e-mail without permission? Sometimes that's the only way that parents can find out about children's illicit materials. Do the ends justify the means?

When dealing with the computer, you need to apply the same principles that you would in terms of eavesdropping on a conversation or looking through your child's dresser drawers, closets, or other private spaces for signs of substance abuse or other activities that could prove harmful.

A related issue concerns the way in which you've positioned computing in your household. Like driving, recreational computing should be regarded as a privilege, not an inalienable right. With privileges, of course, come responsibilities. Stress that your child has the responsibility to live up to the same standards at the keyboard that he or she strives for day by day outside your home. You have the responsibility of ensuring your children's safety, and if that means occasional monitoring of the machine, just as we're all monitored by law enforcement officials when we're on the road, then so be it.

Make your intentions known before you do your first hard-disk sweep, and you'll deflect accusations that Big Brother is looking over everyone's shoulder as they compute. When you do check your hard drive, look for programs that you don't recall purchasing or installing; they could be anything from useful utilities to games you find inappropriate. Look, too, for files that end with .GIF or .JPG, the two most commonly used formats for downloadable photographs. While there's nothing inherently wrong with GIF or JPEG files (they're simply graphic file formats), their sudden proliferation might be a warning light. Look and see, then act accordingly.

## *Set Limits; Draw Boundaries*

It's certainly prudent to carefully monitor and regulate anything that has the potential to chew up vast quantities of your children's time; when we don't set limits from the beginning, the situation becomes increasingly harder to control. Again, consider television. When it first became popular, no one could have imagined that the new wonder technology would become so addictive. By the time people began realizing that TV had become a major—and largely negative—force in our society, it was too late. During the mid-eighties, the average American family was watching more than seven hours of television a day; the average child was getting a daily dose of four to five hours of the plug-in drug each day. Somehow, television escaped the bounds of parenting and took on a life of its own. Today, battles over television with young children have become some of the most difficult to fight, and parents often simply cave into children's demands, rather than endure the pain of implementing change.

So when it comes to recreational computing, when is enough enough? How much time should a child be spending on a computer? There is no right or wrong answer; what works in one household may be too much or too little in another; common sense should prevail. I once heard a computer expert explaining how thrilled he was that his children could spend six or more hours a day focused on the computer; there was not enough focus in most kids' lives, he insisted. I think that the only thing a child needs to do for six or more hours at a stretch is sleep. So to me, there is an amount of computing time that's just plain excessive. At the same time there's a range of computing time that works for any given family.

It's also important to recognize that what works for a middle school child will probably be inappropriate for a high school child. As children get older, they'll use the computer to write papers, conduct research, and crunch numbers; in other words, they'll be using the computer as a productivity tool. That's far different than a younger child playing games or browsing through home reference software or playing with edutainment software, or a very young child just mousing around toddlerware.

Here's a simple formula for helping you decide what amount of computing time is appropriate for your family. Again, the idea of using the formula isn't to derive the correct answer; it's to help you think about valuing and maximizing your child's discretionary time.

## *Bennett's Subtractive Principle*

1. Determine the number of hours between the time your child gets out of school and bedtime.
2. Subtract time for snacks, meals, after-school activities, homework, and bedtime rituals.
3. What you have left probably isn't a whole lot of time, even for a younger child. But whatever the quantity of time may be, ask yourself, "What percentage of that time would be well spent in front of a computer screen?"

In our household, the formula works as follows for a typical day:

> Six hours between school and bedtime minus three hours for extracurricular activities, homework, meals, and bedtime preparation yields three hours of discretionary time.

We allow our kids to compute for a maximum of an hour a day (two half-hour segments), which represents about 33 percent of their free time (we allow more on weekends). In fact, they rarely use two segments a day, even though we don't allow for banking unused computer time. When the timer goes off, our kids know that they have about five minutes to save what they're doing, or conclude an activity and gracefully exit. As they get older and begin using the computer as a tool, those limits will expand. But for a seven- and a ten-year-old, an hour a day seems like ample time at the keyboard.

# *Set Standards for Computer Usage*

## Younger Kids

Once you've set limits for how much time your kids will spend on the computer, the next step is to decide what's acceptable during their time-sanctioned stint at the machine. These usage standards really depend on the child's age. For example, a young child aimlessly mousing around an exploration or activity program and making the same character or object go *boink* for the five hundredth time isn't making very good use of the program. At that point, the computer is reduced to being a device somewhere below television; at least things on the TV keep changing. When you see or hear repetitive action on the screen to the exclusion of anything else, it's time to switch software programs or get involved with the computer session.

## Discussing Online-Stranger Danger with Older Children

We've all heard about the dangers of meeting strangers online. And we all work hard to help our kids recognize dangerous situations with strangers without feeling generally paranoid. We need to explain to our kids that in cyberspace everyone is faceless, and without visual cues and body language, it's hard to know exactly whom you're dealing with via e-mail or in a chat room. And while it's sometimes fun and enlightening to experiment with different personae, some people use that freedom as a source of power for manipulating others. So you need some ground rules, including the following:

1. Never give your real name, phone number, address, or school information to anyone online. Don't provide phony information, either, because you'd be compromising the safety of the person with the substituted name, phone number, or address. Simply use your screen name—nothing more, nothing less.

2. Don't answer questions about your body; if someone seems to be asking untoward questions, tell us or another adult.

3. Never set up in-person meetings with people you meet online. Tell us if someone wants to arrange such a get-together.

The online services also have excellent information about child safety in cyberspace. Read it for more details.

## Shaping Online Behavior of Older Children

As your kids get older, their computing issues, and your challenges and responsibilities, will change. One consideration will be games; what kinds of games are acceptable in your household? Which ones support or contradict your values? Your rules for the types of games your child plays on the computer should complement whatever rules you've established for television, tapes, video games, audio CDs, and movies. You need to make explicit rules about what your children can and can't do in the way of electronic entertainment during their recreational computing time.

Finally, it's important to set standards for what your child may download from newsgroups, Web sites, and bulletin boards. In some cases, this means having that difficult talk with your child about why you don't want pornographic material in the household, and why pornography is so harmful to women in particular and society in general.

You might also consider deploying filtering or blocking software to prevent your child from viewing certain sites. The problem is that the software can block legitimate sites, depending on how it's doing the filtering. For instance, sites that use the word *sex* in the context of gender could be blocked just as easily as sites that offer pornographic materials. The use of filtering software has launched a heated debate on censorship, free speech, government regulation of the Internet, and the rights of organizations to use blocking techniques to advance their own political and social agendas.

From my perspective, what's missing in all the discussion is the responsibility of parents in determining what's acceptable for viewing. As parents, we make rules about how our kids may dress, what they may eat, what kinds of magazines they may bring home, and whom they may bring home. When our kids are out of the house, we hope that they'll abide by the rules and respect our values. If they don't, we take appropriate action. Why not do the same when it comes to dealing with cyberporn? Granted, the easy access makes it more of an issue. But the principles are still the same, and the solution is relatively simple: co-surf with younger kids or be near enough to the computer to see what they're into, and be explicit with older kids about your expectations when they access the Net.

Sometimes this means having an uncomfortable talk with your preteen or teen. As one parent relayed to me during a radio talk show about cybersmut, "I was playing cat and mouse with my son. He was trying to hide fairly raunchy pictures he'd found at a site, and I happened to walk in and see what was on the screen. So we had a talk about obscenity and pornography, just like my father did with me after he discovered some adult magazine sticking out from under my bed. It was kind of a rite of passage."

As with this father, getting started on such a talk can be uncomfortable or embarrassing. Medfield, Massachusetts-based family therapist Carleton Kendrick, has helped numerous parents deal with their children's sexuality issues. According to Kendrick, "Kids visit sex sites for two reasons: (1) They are curious about forbidden fruits, and (2) they want to be sexually excited. Boys cruise sex sites much more than do girls. Boys are trained to view sex in an exclusively genital sense and virtually all pornography is designed to appeal to that genital sexual orientation. My teenage son has informed me that all his male friends know where the sex sites are and keep themselves updated on new sites."

The Internet, Kendrick points out, has made it easy and embarrassment-free to get forbidden sexual content. It's anonymous. It's sometimes free. And it's available twenty-four hours a day, seven days a week. Before the Internet, a school-age child had to risk being seen in public buying a pornographic magazine or trying to rent an X-rated video. You don't have to encounter a soul, however, when you peruse sexual materials on the Internet.

Before talking with your children about sex sites or other objectionable sites (violent or racist, for example), Kendrick strongly suggests viewing the sites yourselves. "It shows you did your homework and that you can't be dismissed with 'You don't know what you're talking about, they're not that bad.' " The alternative is to base your case on news stories or hearsay, which tends to be inaccurate or overstated. Without firsthand knowledge, you'll instantly lose credibility when you make a factual misstatement.

As Kendrick points out, the issue of children's sexuality and the Internet is a delicate one for both parents and children; it's easier simply to avoid the issue than to try to convey your concerns or to set ground rules. He suggests the following guidelines for cybersex discussions with your children:

1. Frame your discussion in the context of your family's overall values: "We don't welcome anything into our home that degrades others. You know that. We don't bring books or movies into our home that promote violence, hatred, and prejudice and we won't allow our computer to be used to bring pictures or words that degrade sex into our home."
2. Acknowledge and be understanding of your children's sexual curiosity, while stating your values regarding sex (before you speak, be sure you can convey comfortably your beliefs and values about sex): "We know you're curious about sex; that's normal. You know we believe sex is a wonderful expression of love between two mature people who share a committed relationship."
3. Tell your children you have formed your opinions and rules based on your actually having visited several Internet sex sites: "We visited these sites to see for ourselves how they portray sex. They treat it in an ugly, impersonal manner, and that's unacceptable."
4. Engage your children in an open-ended discussion as to whether you should install censoring software. Allow

them to voice their opinion: "We can buy software that can block these sex sites and other sites we disapprove of. Do you think we should do that? Would it make things easier for everyone?"

Showing that you empathize with your children's sexual curiosity, and that you haven't forgotten what it's like to be a kid struggling with sex, spares your children any unnecessary embarrassment or humiliation. You can use this cybersex discussion as an opportunity to state (or restate) your views regarding sex and love while asking your children to respect the family's sexual values.

Finally, Kendrick stresses that talks with your children about cybersex will be easier if discussions of sexuality have been taking place at all ages and developmental stages of your children's lives. "Having a discussion of Internet sex sites should not be your first or last discussion of sex with your children," he says. "Your children should be aware of your values regarding sex long before they are aware of sex sites. Because sexuality is such a powerful, scary, confusing issue for kids, parents need to overcome their own discomfort and provide their children with clear guidance, values, and information on this topic. We can't let the Internet pornographers (or TV, movies, and magazines) teach our children the meaning and value of sex."

# Tools for Setting Standards:
# The ABC Method

In Chapter 6, I discussed the nature of rating systems and their limitations. Ultimately, you're the only one who can rate software—and online sites—for their appropriateness in the context of your household. Here's another simple approach that works well for rating television programs and can be applied to computer content as well.

*A-Level:* This includes software and Web sites that reinforce the values of your family in terms of human interactions and conflict resolution, enhance your children's knowledge base, and reward your kids for using their brains and creativity.

*B-Level:* This includes software and Web sites that don't necessarily have redeeming value or don't represent the best use of your children's time. But, at the same time, they don't contradict your values, either.

*C-Level:* This includes software and Web sites that clearly violate your values in terms of language, sexuality, or violence—materials you'd deem off-limits in any other medium as well.

As you allocate your children's time on the computer, you'll obviously want to introduce as many A-level choices as possible. Simply ban the C-level software and sites as unacceptable—period. The C-level rating will no doubt cause the greatest strife in your household, which is why it's important to identify B-levels; you can always use them to counterbalance the Cs you've taken away. Therapist Kendrick suggests that whatever you do, it's important not to humiliate or condemn your children for wanting to play sexually oriented or violent games, or for spending time playing games and visiting sites that are essentially mind-numbing: "Your kids are merely responding with age-appropriate sexual curiosity, an appetite for violence unfortunately encouraged by our culture, and a desire to 'waste time' or 'chill out' by doing something mindless."

In discussing your opinions and allowances of Internet sites and computer games you have an opportunity to demonstrate your strongly held values on sex, violence, intolerance and being "dumbed down," Kendrick comments. "It's also a chance to model the fine art of empathic argument, negotiation, and compromise. Remember, this is not a battle to be won or lost. It's a time to further clarify what your family stands for."

## Dealing with "Slice 'em and Dice 'em" Programs

Computer game makers churn out endless violent software (designed to appeal to boys) featuring gratuitous torture, maiming, and murder. After playing some of these gore-ridden games yourselves, you may be horrified enough to ban them from your home. Be sure to look at the computer gaming magazines that your child might purchase or want to subscribe to, as well. They can be worse than the games themselves, and often feature strategy articles designed to help your child become a more effective and savage on-screen killer. The ads in the magazines often sport headlines like "Violent, sadistic, and has no redeeming moral value. No wonder it was voted game of the year." They promise sensationalistic gore: "After you crash we simply hose the pulpy red mess off the dash and give the car to the next guy." And they goad kids on with phrases like "Do you have what it takes to be a superhero?" and "If you've got the balls, we've got the ballistics." Here are some tips on violent-game-proofing your computer and discussing it with your children:

1. Explain your prohibition of violent computer games to your children in the context of your overall family values: "We don't condone or celebrate cruelty or violence of any kind in this family. If we let you play these senseless games of slaughter and called it fun, we would be hypocrites and our family's values regarding violence would be lies."

2. Acknowledge the peer pressure to play these games: "We believe you when you say all your friends play these games. We know it's hard sometimes to be the kids whose uncool parents won't let them do the popular thing. We think it's more important to stand up for your beliefs than to go along with the crowd."

3. Play some of these violent games yourselves. Your opinions and arguments will be more respected: "I don't think games that encourage and reward you for tearing out people's beating hearts or for chopping off their heads are funny or healthy. You can't see the connection now between your playing these games and your becoming insensitive to violence. We can and we don't approve of anything that could affect you like that."

4. Always remain open to discuss the appropriateness of vi-

olence in a computer game: "If there are games with violence in them that you think I might approve of, show
them to me and we'll discuss why you may or may not
play them."

## *My Favorite Waste of Time*

If you find yourselves forbidding your children the use of
the computer for mindless entertainment, check out your
own use of leisure time. How many of your leisure activities
have an A-level rating? Do your TV watching, computing,
reading, and hobbies all have educational value?

Spending hours daily playing veg-out computer games is
as unhealthy as zoning out for hours every day in front of
the TV. But kids deserve some mindless downtime too, on
occasion, to unwind from their all-too-hectic schedules.
Telling your kids they can use the computer only for educational pursuits is a great way to dampen their computing en-
thusiasm and exploration. The occasional use of the
computer for pure fun and relaxation is harmless. We all
need vacations from school, don't we?

## *Be Realistic About Your Sphere of Influence*

One question I'm often asked is how we control computer
usage when our children visit friends' homes. Simple. We
don't! Same with television watching. If you ask a neighbor
to adhere to the same rules that you do around computers
and television watching, you immediately create an us-

versus-them situation: "Oh, we don't play that kind of game at our house," "We don't let the guys play on the computer the whole afternoon," and so on. The reality is that you can control what happens within the four walls of your house, but no farther. At some point, you have to trust that the values and codes of behavior you've tried to teach have sunk in, and that your children will behave away from home (physically or in cyberspace) as you have taught them.

Besides, if your child does wind up spending five hours at a friend's house playing on the computer, or perhaps playing games you wouldn't have in your own home, you're far better off if your child feels he or she can be honest with you. Use the occurrence as an opportunity to point out all the other things your child could have been doing with the friend, and discuss the price that he or she paid for devoting the entire afternoon to recreational computing. It's always better, in the long run, if you create an environment in which your child can speak openly with you.

However you go about getting involved and setting limits for computer use in your own home, you'll find the benefits are many. First, you'll ensure that the computer doesn't overrun your child's life, and that longtime hobbies and interests don't go by the wayside. You'll also be teaching an important lesson in self-regulation, which will benefit your children in other areas of life, too. Finally, you'll find that traditional activities will likely resurface on their own as your children go about the business of being kids while being digital.

# *Summary*

Set goals for yourself regarding involvement with your kids' computing, and be willing to serve as a role model yourself. Setting standards for the computer might seem difficult, but you've already done just that for other media and other pursuits. Tackle the tough stuff with honest talk. You might just find it an opportunity to discuss those prickly issues you've dreaded bringing to the table. Finally, be firm but gentle if there's backsliding; this is a new realm for you and your kids. Think of yourself as a pioneer in this new technological world. You might not have asked for the job, but it's an important part of parenting these days. And it will only become more so as the digital age unfolds.

# Postscript:
# In the Wake of the Quake

Much has changed since I began writing this book. Dozens of high-quality learning tools, reference tools, and creativity-sparking games have come to market. So have more violent games; Quake is now an anachronism in terms of action games, having been superceded by Quake II and others. Before the ink on this paper dries, Quake II will no doubt be outdone by something else that pushes the envelope of imaginative bodily destruction.

On a brighter note, in some respects cyberspace has gotten better. It's considerably easier to find information than it was a year ago. New tools and technologies are bringing the Web into its own as an exciting new medium for conveying ideas and information in a novel way. Many site designers and content providers have figured out the art of presenting information in ways that take advantage of the Web's unique potential. Also, more learning institutions, museums, zoos, and libraries have gained a strong Web presence; we've almost come to expect that every resource in the real world will have a Web counterpart.

Despite the improvements and the availability of search tools, the Web still has its problems. Amidst the gems, it's littered with useless or dubious information, dead sites, and promotional materials. And while much of the formerly free smut is now pay-for-view smut, the Web is still a potential source for troubling materials. Rating systems, filtering systems, censorship, and government regulation of cyberspace will continue to be the source of fierce debates, leaving parents to their own devices.

In short, as the dream machine has become even more promising, the digital demon will continue to work its mischief. I suspect this trend will continue for many years; never has such powerful electronic technology been placed in the hands of the consuming public with so little thought as to its potential effects, good and bad.

Still, I believe that the basic parentware principles I've described in this book will remain relevant for years to come, whatever the nature of the technology at hand. After all, the principles revolve around fundamental parenting issues, such as setting limits, creating boundaries, keeping informed, and staying connected.

As the digital age evolves, we'll undoubtedly find ourselves facing new challenges and opportunities for applying good parentware. Take videoconferencing. For years, soothsayers have predicted that videotelephones will become standard household gear (think of all the sci-fi movies in which the videophone is a prop). It will probably be a while before your basic phone includes a built-in camera and monitor. But personal videoconferencing, which allows people to send live images of themselves to others while they talk, is here today and getting more affordable by the month. It's not unreasonable to envision computers or monitors that contain built-in cameras sometime in the not-so-distant future; as a general rule, certain peripherals become internals as they become more popular and more a part of everyday work. (Consider items such as CD-ROMs, tape backup, and modems—the first models were clunky externals. Now they're standard gear supplied inside the machines.) When videoconferencing becomes widely available, we'll clearly need to teach our kids how to effectively use this exciting new form of communication.

Then there's the old "one-eyed monster" issue. The Web is already proving to be a compelling alternative to television. Compelling, in the sense that the production values, sights, sounds, animations, and video quality will rival those of TV. The programming, too, will eclipse the offerings on the tube; thousands of "stations" will be there to view with the click of a mouse. In addition to concerns about content appropriateness, people also have concerns that the Web may spawn a generation of "keyboard potatoes." And to prevent the Web from becoming a major time sink, we'll need to apply the best parentware techniques that we can.

The list of prognostications could continue for pages. But the central point is that the rapid evolution of electronic technology is having a tangible and profound effect on how our kids live and learn. Perhaps it all seems to be happening too fast. Perhaps things seem out of control. But remember, no matter what the technology of the day may be, we're still empowered to help our children lead balanced and safe lives and enjoy the best of what technology has to offer.

# Appendix:
# Content-Filtering Software

Cybersitter. Solid Oak Software Inc. 800-388-2761 (www. cybersitter.com)

Cyber Patrol. The Learning Company, 617-494-1200 (www.cyberpatrol.com)

Cyber Snoop, Pearl Software Inc. 800-732-7596 (www. pearlsw.com)

Net Nanny, Net Nanny Ltd., 800-340-7177 (www.netnanny. com)

SurfWatch, SurfWatch Software Inc., 800-458-6600 (www. surfwatch.com)

WebChaperone, WebCo International Inc., 800-387-8373 (www.webchaperone.com)

# Acknowledgments

This book would not have happened without the help and encouragement of a number of people. First of all, my deep appreciation to Stacey Miller, a world-class writer, researcher, and editor. Many, many thanks for your incredibly hard work and perserverance on this project. Thanks too, go to Pete Scisco, for his technical advice, to Deborah Kovacs and Ellen Goldberg for sharing their knowledge of the Net with me, and to Carleton Kendrick for offering his insights into kids and media. Dr. Richard Venezky was kind enough to share his ideas and conclusions with me, as was Dr. Susan Haugland.

I very much appreciate the hard work that Tracy Smith, my editor at Times Books/Random House, put into the manuscript. Thanks for your patience and guidance, Trace. And thanks to my current editor, John Rambow, for helping to carry the project over the finish line. In addition, I'd like to thank Lynn Chu and Glen Hartley for handling the business end of this project.

I owe a debt to my wife, Ruth, for serving as a sounding board for my parenting observations and for contributing many of her own ideas and insights. Finally, hats off to my children, Noah and Audrey, for putting up with my silly questions while they ran their favorite programs. Now that the book is done, I'll try not to interrupt again—at least for a while.

# Index

# About the Author

STEVE BENNETT is a full-time author who has written more than fifty-five books in the fields of computing, parenting, environment, and business. He is the coauthor, with his wife, Ruth, of the bestselling *365 TV-Free Activities You Can Do with Your Child*. He also pens @home.computing, a syndicated page that includes software reviews, online site reviews, and his award-winning column, "Parentware." Steve has contributed to numerous publications, including *Computer Life, SmartComputing,* and *Family Circle's Computers Made Easy.* Steve holds a master's degree in regional studies from Harvard University.